CREATING RELEVANCE IN A TIME OF UNCERTAINTY

How to Create Deep,
Lasting, and Mutually Satisfying
Relationships With the
People Who Keep You in Business

ANDREA COVILLE,

Chief Executive Officer, Brodeur Partners

with **PAUL B. BROWN**

ISBN 978-1-09835-963-8

Because this book was written in most part during the early months of the pandemic, I would like to dedicate it to all creatures great and small who kept us company and kept us calm. In particular, to my faithful friend Cooper, who will have a place under my desk and in my heart, forever.

Contents

Contents

SECTION I.
HOW TO CREATE RELEVANCE

Introduction

We were just putting the finishing touches on this book when the COVID-19 pandemic hit. Hundreds of thousands of people died. Financial markets were in disarray, and in the U.S. alone, about one-fourth of the workforce had filed for unemployment. Months later, we had a presidential election. During the campaign, we saw the impact of the lack of civil discourse and viewed in stark relief just how divided Americans are in their political beliefs. Trust has diminished, and we have seen communities become more polarized, particularly online.

That's the big picture. But there are some subtle—and important—shifts among generations involving what is relevant to them today and moving forward. It is vital for communicators, and the ideas and brands they represent, to understand the linkages among communities (tribes) and to make a commitment to authentic words and deeds. Never has it been harder to build relevance, but it has also never been a more significant opportunity.

We have seen that in times of uncertainty, people do one of three things:

1. They panic.

2. They ignore what is going on in the hope that they will not be affected.

3. They engage.

Obviously, we think you should engage. How you can do that is what this book is all about.

1

How This Book Can Help You

It doesn't matter what you do for a living. You can be the CEO of a Fortune 100 company, a senior marketer, someone working at a small firm, an entrepreneur, or a leader at a nonprofit. Your position doesn't matter. Here's what does: We all want to connect with our customers.

On one level, of course, that's just Marketing 101. If you haven't connected with potential customers and they really don't know you exist, you can't get them to buy your product or service or adopt your point of view. And they won't know you exist unless you interact with them somehow. Without that engagement, there is no chance you are ever going to create the connection you need to influence someone's thoughts and/or actions.

And so, the takeaway is clear: *No matter what we do for a living, we all want to connect with our customers and the people we would like to be our customers.*

But the desire to forge that relationship, that bond, goes beyond our need to conduct transactions or persuade people. It is deeper than that. Most of us are proud of the work we do. We think the products we sell, or the services we offer, have value. (And if we are employed by the government or a nonprofit, we believe we really are in a position to make people's lives better.)

However, none of that does any good if people don't know we exist. The best medical clinic in the world is of absolutely no value if those in need of care don't go there because they have never heard of it. And a product, service, or point of view that could make someone's life better *won't*, if the people who could benefit don't know about it.

But again, they won't know about what we have unless our offering, message, or idea resonates.

Communication must quickly and obviously meet your audience's needs. What you are sharing or selling cannot be about you—the person/company communicating—it has to be about what is important to the people you are trying to reach.

What could keep your message from getting through? You know the list as well as we do. It divides into three parts: the number of messages each of us receives every day, the time pressure we all are under, and most recently, the lack of trust we have in nearly everything.

Let's deal with the sheer volume of messages first. There are the commercial ones—television commercials, paid social, influencer campaigns, radio spots, print ads, and the various other ways people try to grab our attention online—but there are also tweets, posts, texts, and videos. And that's just in our limited spare time (more on that in a minute).

At work, and that includes the fact that tens of millions of us are now working from home, we get communications from all directions: emails, memos, voicemails, company publications and reports, sales updates, and industry trade publications. The list seems endless and ever-increasing.

The total number of messages we receive is enormous, and there is no way we can pay attention to each one.

And the reason we can't is because of the time pressure we are all under. Know anyone who has said recently, "I just don't know what I am going to do with myself today," or "I have a couple of hours to kill.'"? We don't either. When you feel you don't have any time to waste—because you don't—you are only going to pay attention to the messages that are most important to you.

LET'S CATCH OUR BREATH

Let's pause for a moment to see where all that time pressure is coming from. In our pandemic-driven Zoom culture, where home has become the workplace for many, there are fewer boundaries and longer days.

As the economy tries to recover, organizations continue to hire the absolute minimum number of people. We all are working harder and are under more stress, which is yet another reason we will only pay attention to the most vital messages. The need for mental health has overtaken physical health for Millennials and Gen Xers, the groups who have seen the most significant financial impact from the pandemic.

Not only has the steady rise of two-income families increased time stress, but many of today's young parents find themselves concerned about their career paths. And as with prior generations, they are increasingly having to help out with their parents, in addition to raising their own kids. Again, that leaves little time to waste.

The net result? The people you are trying to reach are reluctant—and often downright unreceptive—to what you have to say. They resent that you are trying to distract them from things that they consider to be more important.

And the fact that so many of the messages we receive come from people and organizations with a particular bias (and are therefore suspect from a trust point of view) just makes things worse.

RELEVANCE

WHAT YOU HAVE TO DO

After everything we just talked about, the obvious question to ask is: how do you connect to people at this moment in time. How do you begin to form a relationship so that they will pay attention to what you have to offer or say? And most importantly, how can you create a relationship that is built on trust and will last?

In our last book, we laid out the starting point. You need to be relevant.

Webster's defines relevance as *being practically and especially socially applicable.* And we think that's right, although we have found most people misread the definition and put the emphasis on the practical. It is certainly true that what you are offering must solve a customer need and do it well.

But increasingly, that is not enough. The time-pressed and stressed people you are trying to reach are becoming progressively discerning. For example, if you ask them if they want high quality or a good price, they will answer "yes" every time. They expect superior execution on your part. That is the price of entry, no matter what your organization does, and (unfortunately) not even that guarantees a long-term relationship. A slip, or an encounter with someone who does what you do slightly better, or just as well at a lower price, and the relationship could be over.

And that is where the emotional part of relevance, what Webster's called "the especially socially applicable," comes in. If your product/service/idea resonates with a customer, if it means something to them—in addition to being utilitarian—then the relationship will be deeper, longer-lasting, and more profitable.

You will have formed the connection we talked about.

It also explains why they will stay with you. It is easy to switch to another brand, company, product, or service unless people feel some sort of personal connection to your offering.

> Everything is personal.

That's why relevance is so important. Unlike other objectives marketers have aspired to—e.g., engagement, "eyeballs," alignment, buzz, and clicks—only relevance has the power to change not only people's minds but their actions as well.

In "**Relevance**: The Power to Change Minds and Behavior and Stay Ahead of the Competition," we talked about this at a high, i.e., strategic level. (And if you haven't read **Relevance**, no worries. We will reprise the central argument in Chapter 2.)

Marketing, as you know, is "simply" figuring out who you want to sell to and then determining what will get those people to buy.

By that definition, our first book concentrated on the back half of the equation. How can you get people to buy? And the answer was: by being relevant.

Here, we are going to approach the question from the other end: **Who can you reach using relevance?**

Having done that, we will go on to talk about tactics and how you can forge relationships with customers—and the people you would like to be your customers—to get the results you need.

WHERE WE ARE GOING

We will go into all of this in detail in the pages ahead, but let us foreshadow the argument here.

Your starting point is understanding what is important to the people you are trying to reach, so you can engage with them using the lens through which they view the world.

This is an extremely important point. The world feels uncertain at the moment for many, so **you need to start from the place where they already are.**

As you will see, our socially distanced, overwhelmed, time-pressed customers use filters to decide how they engage with marketers.

Specifically, there are eight filters that divide into four quadrants. Sometimes your potential customer will use just one of them to decide whether they will pay attention to what you have to say. Sometimes they will use two or three or all four quadrants.

Those filters?

Thinking

The filters here are totally rational.

People ask:

- Does this help me meet my needs?

- Could it make my life easier?

Community

These filters deal with opportunities to connect and interact.

People ask:

- Does being associated with this make me feel better about myself? Or they say:

- I want people to know I am associated with it.

Values

The values filters align with what people stand for and what they believe.

People say:

- I associate the message/idea with principles that are important to me.

- It stands for the same things I do.

Sensory

Sensory filters deal with our emotions.

People say:

• I like the feeling when I'm around it.

• It inspires me.

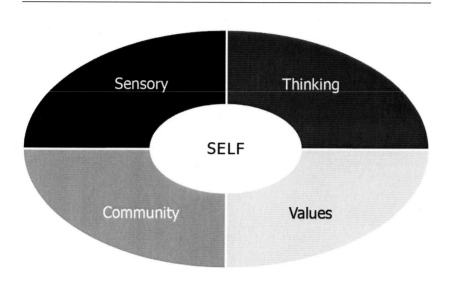

Your message (and the appeal of your product or service) must make it through one of these eight filters if you are going to be heard and listened to. We will give you case studies to show you how your peers have implemented each and every one of them in Section II of the book.

Reaching and engaging people today is harder than it has ever been, as you well know. We promise that what you will read in the pages ahead will make it easier.

Let's begin.

2

What's New?

Back in 2012, we launched the Brodeur Relevance Model, which focuses on the four ways a person connects with a brand, product, service, or cause. The four quadrants: thinking, community, values, and sensory experience.

We have updated our findings periodically ever since, and you will discover our latest findings throughout.

Below is a sample:

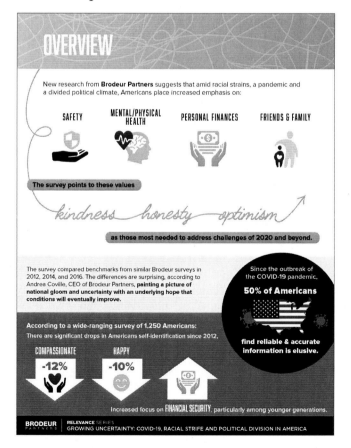

RELEVANCE

But let us foreshadow what you are about to read. The current data reinforces the stability of the Brodeur Relevance Model; most of the data is relatively unchanged since we began.

For example, take a look at the response to the question below, asking people what they value. You'll see a lot of movement in the chart, but when you look at the actual numbers, you realize that they really didn't change very much during the intervening eight years.

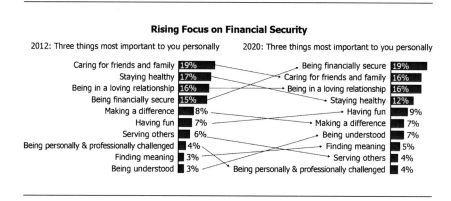

Rising Focus on Financial Security

2012: Three things most important to you personally

2020: Three things most important to you personally

That isn't surprising. Values and how people interact with brands, products, and services are unlikely to change quickly.

But they do change.

And the current shifts that appear to be happening are in the areas of (shared) **values** and **community**. Specifically, the data suggests that people are putting more emphasis on those factors.

What's New?

Just look at the following chart:

Uptick in People Focusing on Shared Values and Community

For each of the following, please select whether this mostly describes you or whether this mostly does not describe you.

Question Type: Single Matrix | Total Respondents: 1,250

Sensory: + 3% (average)
What experiences are most meaningful and inspiring?

Describes me extremely or very well	2016	2020
Believes how something makes you "feel" is as important as its practical utility	40%	43%
Easily affected by strong emotions	42%	41%
Makes decisions based on gut instinct	35%	37%
Chooses a "fun experience" over what others consider practical	26%	34%

Thinking: -5% (average)
What tangible needs will have the most impact right now?

Describes me extremely or very well	2016	2020
A practical person	67%	62%
When solving problems, you usually take the most rational choice	62%	58%
Methodical in evaluating things	54%	51%
Analyzes and always chooses the optimal value	56%	50%

Sensory | Thinking
SELF
Community | Values

Community: + 11% (average)
What connections and interactions make you feel better about yourself?

Describes me extremely or very well	2016	2020
Easily empathize with the concerns of others	59%	57%
When making decisions, you look to others for advice	18%	33%
Before doing something, you always check with others	15%	30%
Relies on the advice of colleagues	13%	29%

Values: + 6% (average)
What values do you want to stand for in these times?

Describes me extremely or very well	2016	2020
Most friends share your political, cultural, & social values	26%	42%
Actions are frequently influenced by beliefs and values	63%	56%
Goes out of way to support things you believe in	48%	49%
Regularly pay more for ethical products and services	18%	32%

This may be a good sign for cause-marketing and movement-based campaigns. However, it also appears to reflect a balkanization and self-separation of communities based on political, social, and moral beliefs.

RELEVANCE

You can see that when we compare our latest results to what we found four years earlier.

There are other changes, as well. We will flag them as we proceed through the book, but let's touch on them here.

The effects of the pandemic and civil unrest following the death of George Floyd in 2020. Three things jumped out at us about this from the research.

Values. People believe that what will pull us through the tough times we face are American values rooted in kindness, honesty, and optimism.

Values We Need: Dealing with Pandemic and Civil Unrest

Top Values Needed in 2020

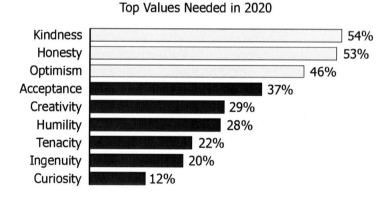

Kindness 54%
Honesty 53%
Optimism 46%
Acceptance 37%
Creativity 29%
Humility 28%
Tenacity 22%
Ingenuity 20%
Curiosity 12%

What the world needs now is kindness, honesty, and optimism.

- Of those three, the most important values that people cited that would help us deal with the challenges of 2020 were kindness and honesty...Both of which often seem in short supply.

- Many of those values associated with American entrepreneurial engagement—tenacity, ingenuity, curiosity—weren't viewed by respondents as things that would most help address what we're facing now.

- Overall, what Americans seem to be saying is that the "softer" and more emotion-related values are what we need to address the problems of today. This may be what we see reflected on streets and on campuses in addressing systemic bias and racism.

Kindness and optimism were in short supply during the COVID-19 crisis, as you can see from the following chart. (Notice the dramatic drop in compassion and happiness.)

RELEVANCE

A More Somber and Sober Mood

Below are a list of labels that are often attached to people. For each, I would like you to rate them as to how well they apply to you. The scale is 0 to 10 with a zero being "does not apply at all" and 10 being "totally applies."

Question Type: Single Matrix | Total Respondents: 1,250

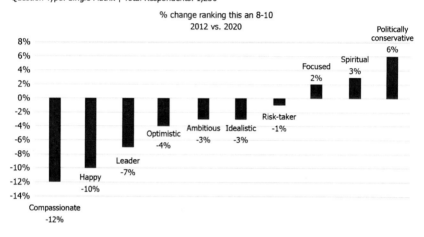

% change ranking this an 8-10
2012 vs. 2020

What's even more alarming about that happiness finding is how the numbers break down generationally. The younger you are, the unhappier you are.

The Happiness Generational Split

How would you assess your own personal happiness and personal fulfillment using a scale of 0-100 with 0 being unhappy and unfulfilled and 100 being extremely happy and fulfilled?

Question Type: Slider Scale | Total Respondents: 1,250

Personal Happiness & Fulfillment	Total All Respondents (n=1,250)	Gender Male (n=622)	Female (n=620)	Generation Gen Z (n=201)	Millennial (n=312)	Gen X (n=287)	Boomer (n=350)	Silent (n=100)
Very happy & very fulfilled (gave rating of 80-100)	48%	49%	48%	31%	39%	54%	58%	60%
Somewhat happy & somewhat fulfilled (gave rating of 30-79)	47%	47%	47%	62%	56%	40%	40%	37%
Not very happy & not very fulfilled (gave rating of 0-29)	5%	4%	5%	7%	5%	6%	2%	3%

Gen Z (15-23) Millennial (24-39) Gen X (40-55) Boomer (55-74) Silent (75+)

Older generations are happier and more fulfilled than younger generations.

Over half of Gen X, Boomer, and Silent Generation members say they are very happy and very fulfilled—only a third of Gen Zers and Millennials feel the same.

Gen Zers and Millennials mostly fall somewhere in the middle, with well over half saying they are only somewhat happy and somewhat fulfilled.

RELEVANCE

Everything is more significant. While everyone agrees with the increased importance of family and physical well-being, younger generations are much more focused on personal finance and careers, as you can see from the following two graphics.

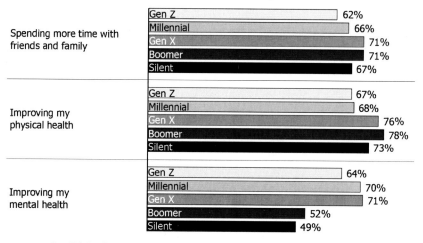

Rising Importance: Older Generations' Focus on Family and Health

% Much more + Somewhat more important

Spending more time with friends and family
- Gen Z — 62%
- Millennial — 66%
- Gen X — 71%
- Boomer — 71%
- Silent — 67%

Improving my physical health
- Gen Z — 67%
- Millennial — 68%
- Gen X — 76%
- Boomer — 78%
- Silent — 73%

Improving my mental health
- Gen Z — 64%
- Millennial — 70%
- Gen X — 71%
- Boomer — 52%
- Silent — 49%

Gen Z (15-23) Millennial (24-39) Gen X (40-55) Boomer (55-74) Silent (75+)

Everyone is interested in health and family. But underneath that lies differences depending on how old you are.

If you're a Boomer or older (age 55+), you are more likely to be focused on health and family.

Rising Importance: Younger Generation's Focus on Finance & Career

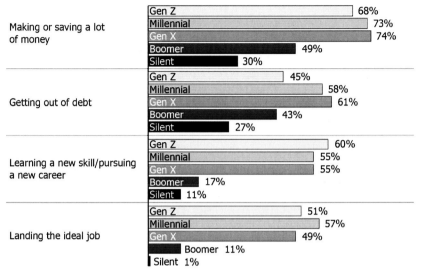

% Much more + Somewhat more important

Making or saving a lot of money
- Gen Z: 68%
- Millennial: 73%
- Gen X: 74%
- Boomer: 49%
- Silent: 30%

Getting out of debt
- Gen Z: 45%
- Millennial: 58%
- Gen X: 61%
- Boomer: 43%
- Silent: 27%

Learning a new skill/pursuing a new career
- Gen Z: 60%
- Millennial: 55%
- Gen X: 55%
- Boomer: 17%
- Silent: 11%

Landing the ideal job
- Gen Z: 51%
- Millennial: 57%
- Gen X: 49%
- Boomer: 11%
- Silent: 1%

Gen Z (15-23) Millennial (24-39) Gen X (40-55) Boomer (55-74) Silent (75+)

Not so if you're a Millennial or Gen Xer (age 24-55). For them, making or saving money is more or at least as important as their physical or mental health.

Ditto on career development, which barely registers for Boomers but ranks high among Gen Zers, Millennials, and Gen Xers.

RELEVANCE

Finding truth. At the top of the list of things becoming "more difficult" is getting access to reliable information. Obviously, that is not a good thing when a society is dealing with a pandemic. It adds stress.

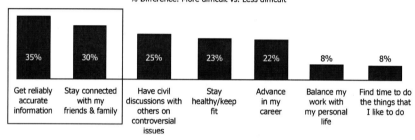

Rising Difficulty: Getting Reliably Accurate Information

Compared to six months ago, are the following becoming easier for you or more difficult for you?

Question Type: Single Matrix | Total Respondents: 1,250

% Difference: More difficult vs. Less difficult

Get reliably accurate information	Stay connected with my friends & family	Have civil discussions with others on controversial issues	Stay healthy/keep fit	Advance in my career	Balance my work with my personal life	Find time to do the things that I like to do
35%	30%	25%	23%	22%	8%	8%

The most notable gaps in things that are becoming more or less difficult for Americans are getting reliably accurate information and staying connected with friends and family.

There is a smaller, but notable, gap in having civil discussions, staying healthy, and advancing careers.

There's less of a stark difference in balancing work with personal life and finding time to do things they like.

What's New?

Digging a little deeper, we can see that there are two huge sources of stress for Millennials and Gen Xers: advancing in their careers and trying to achieve a work-life balance.

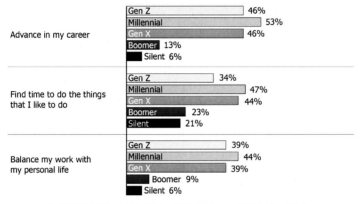

Rising Difficulty: Career and Work-life Balance

Compared to six months ago, are the following becoming easier for you or more difficult for you?
Question Type: Single Matrix | Total Respondents: 1,250

% Much more + Somewhat more difficult

Advance in my career
- Gen Z 46%
- Millennial 53%
- Gen X 46%
- Boomer 13%
- Silent 6%

Find time to do the things that I like to do
- Gen Z 34%
- Millennial 47%
- Gen X 44%
- Boomer 23%
- Silent 21%

Balance my work with my personal life
- Gen Z 39%
- Millennial 44%
- Gen X 39%
- Boomer 9%
- Silent 6%

Gen Z (15-23) Millennial (24-39) Gen X (40-55) Boomer (55-74) Silent (75+)

Stressors for Millennials and Gen Xers center around career and work-life balance.

The main stressors for Millennials and Gen Xers relate to advancing in their careers and balancing that with their personal and family lives. Approximately half say that advancing in their career has become more difficult in the past six months.

These challenges barely register with the over-55 crowd (Boomers & Silents).

RELEVANCE

THE CHALLENGE OF CIVIL DISCOURSE

Two in five Americans say that having civil conversations on issues is now more challenging.

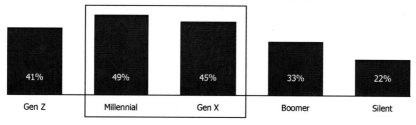

Having Civil Discourse Is Becoming More Difficult

Compared to six months ago, are the following becoming easier for you or more difficult for you?

Question Type: Single Matrix | Total Respondents: 1,250

% Having Civil Conversation Has Become More Difficult

Gen Z	Millennial	Gen X	Boomer	Silent
41%	49%	45%	33%	22%

Gen Z (15-23) Millennial (24-39) Gen X (40-55) Boomer (55-74) Silent (75+)

Having civil conversations is becoming more difficult.

- Two-in-five Americans say that it is becoming more difficult to have civil conversations on controversial issues.

- This is true across generations but is particularly prevalent among Millennials and Gen Xers.

- Engaging in civil discourse is less of a challenge for the low-income, non-college-educated population. Rather, this appears to be more of a challenge with the affluent ($100K+/47%) and more highly educated (post-grad/51%) Americans.

What's New?

A majority of Americans say the main culprit is the internet.

The Challenge of Civil Discourse: Online Acceleration

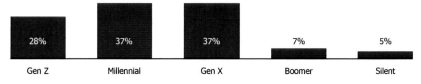

56% Agree the internet has been the main cause for uncivil discourse

% Has written a comment critical of a post on social media at least once a month

28%	37%	37%	7%	5%
Gen Z	Millennial	Gen X	Boomer	Silent

Gen Z (15-23) Millennial (24-39) Gen X (40-55) Boomer (55-74) Silent (75+)

One culprit that most people point to is the internet, which makes it much easier to express criticism.

• Well over half of Americans agree that the internet has been the main cause for uncivil discourse.

• At the same time, many of us admit to contributing to the problem.

  o Half of Americans say they have written comments critical of others' posts on social media.

  o Over one-third of Millennials and Gen Xers say they write critical comments on other peoples' posts at least once a month or more.

  o People who say they post critical comments on others' posts are also more likely to be highly educated (41% of post-graduates) and affluent (36% of those with incomes over $100K).

RELEVANCE

The challenge appears to be the result of a competition between two forces: While Americans believe everyone's views should be respected, they also feel an obligation to speak out on important issues and "correct" people "when they are wrong."

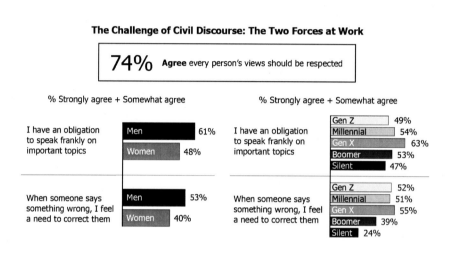

The Challenge of Civil Discourse: The Two Forces at Work

74% **Agree** every person's views should be respected

% Strongly agree + Somewhat agree

I have an obligation to speak frankly on important topics
- Men 61%
- Women 48%

When someone says something wrong, I feel a need to correct them
- Men 53%
- Women 40%

% Strongly agree + Somewhat agree

I have an obligation to speak frankly on important topics
- Gen Z 49%
- Millennial 54%
- Gen X 63%
- Boomer 53%
- Silent 47%

When someone says something wrong, I feel a need to correct them
- Gen Z 52%
- Millennial 51%
- Gen X 55%
- Boomer 39%
- Silent 24%

What follows from this is obvious and unfortunate. There is pushback on both sides of just about every issue, which results in polarization.

The following graphic makes that clear.

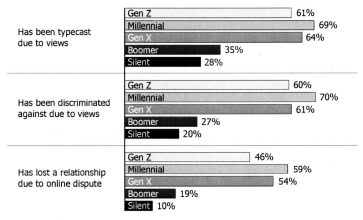

The Civil Discourse Challenge: the Cost is Labeling, Typecasting & Loss of Relationships

% Has happened to them in the last six months

Has been typecast due to views
- Gen Z 61%
- Millennial 69%
- Gen X 64%
- Boomer 35%
- Silent 28%

Has been discriminated against due to views
- Gen Z 60%
- Millennial 70%
- Gen X 61%
- Boomer 27%
- Silent 20%

Has lost a relationship due to online dispute
- Gen Z 46%
- Millennial 59%
- Gen X 54%
- Boomer 19%
- Silent 10%

Gen Z (15-23) Millennial (24-39) Gen X (40-55) Boomer (55-74) Silent (75+)

- Over half of Americans say they have been labeled or typecast as a result of their personal and political views. Half say this has resulted in some form of discrimination.

   o These numbers are much higher among the young. Approximately two-thirds of Millennials and Gen Xers say they have been labeled or typecast for their views. A similar percentage of Millennials and Gen Xers say that has resulted in some form of discrimination.

- This is also costing us relationships. Two-in-five Americans say they've lost or severed a relationship due to an online dispute.

   o Again, these numbers are much higher among Millennials and Gen Xers.

RELEVANCE

Let's discuss one last finding.

CORPORATE SOCIAL RESPONSIBILITY (CSR)

Among the different CSR elements tested, sustainability and environmental responsibility issues are overall the most influential in Americans' purchasing decisions—particularly among the younger generations (Gen Z, Millennial, and Gen X). This is true whether we are talking about expensive luxury purchases, consumer packaged goods, or personal care items.

Labor and human rights policies are second and have particular appeal among women and those over 55.

Which of the following is the most important consideration when considering...?

Question Type: Single Choice | Total Respondents: 1,250

Most important consideration	Total	Gender		Generation				
	2020	Male	Female	Gen Z	Millennial	Gen X	Boomer	Silent
Purchase something expensive								
Policies on environmental & sustainability issues	36%	36%	37%	40%	41%	36%	31%	29%
Labor & human right policies	24%	19%	28%	20%	14%	18%	34%	40%
Purchase general consumer goods								
Policies on environmental & sustainability issues	33%	36%	30%	40%	38%	34%	24%	28%
Labor & human right policies	24%	16%	31%	21%	16%	19%	34%	35%
Purchase a personal item								
Labor & human right policies	31%	24%	39%	29%	16%	22%	47%	55%
Policies on environmental & sustainability issues	28%	31%	25%	27%	36%	33%	19%	23%

Gen Z (15-23) Millennial (24-39) Gen X (40-55) Boomer (55-74) Silent (75+)

> **Among the four corporate social responsibility areas tested, a brand's environmental and sustainability policies are the biggest purchase factors for Gen Z and Millennials.**
>
> • Environmental and sustainability factors were—by far—the most important purchase decisions for Gen Zers and Millennials across all types of purchase decisions—from expensive durable goods to general consumer packaged goods to personal items.
>
> • For these young consumers, labor and workforce issues tended to take a distant second place.

As we said, we will talk about all of this throughout the book and what it means if you want to connect to consumers and customers. But before we move on, let's end the chapter on a positive note—the following graphic.

RELEVANCE

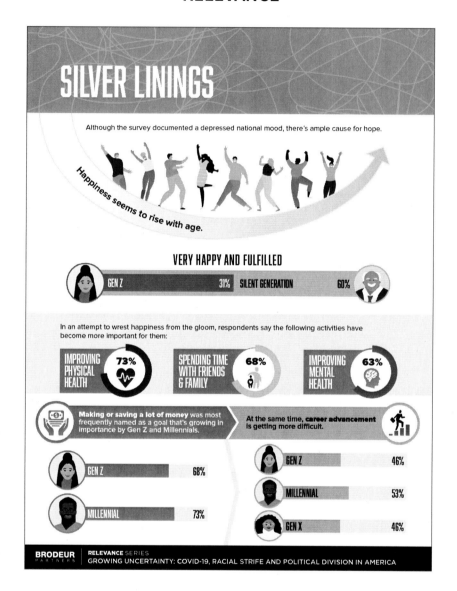

SILVER LININGS

Although the survey documented a depressed national mood, there's ample cause for hope.

Happiness seems to rise with age.

VERY HAPPY AND FULFILLED

GEN Z **31%** SILENT GENERATION **60%**

In an attempt to wrest happiness from the gloom, respondents say the following activities have become more important for them:

IMPROVING PHYSICAL HEALTH **73%**

SPENDING TIME WITH FRIENDS & FAMILY **68%**

IMPROVING MENTAL HEALTH **63%**

Making or saving a lot of money was most frequently named as a goal that's growing in importance by Gen Z and Millennials.

At the same time, **career advancement** is getting more difficult.

GEN Z **68%**

MILLENNIAL **73%**

GEN Z **46%**

MILLENNIAL **53%**

GEN X **46%**

BRODEUR PARTNERS | **RELEVANCE** SERIES
GROWING UNCERTAINTY: COVID-19, RACIAL STRIFE AND POLITICAL DIVISION IN AMERICA

3

Your Customers Are (Even) Smarter Than You Think

As business leaders, marketers, and communicators, we talk all the time about how our messages need to "break through the clutter" to reach our overwhelmed (and over-messaged) customers and potential customers.

Well, guess what? Those customers and potential customers have beaten us to the proverbial punch. They already have figurative—and in some cases, literal—mental filters in place to figure out what they will pay attention to and what they won't. (And this is over and above the spam-type filters that people have in place on their computers and phones.)

What this means is the problem of reaching them is even more difficult than we thought.

Not only are they getting bombarded with far more communications than they could possibly pay attention to—the accepted wisdom is people receive north of 5,000 messages a day—but they have figured out a way to automatically filter out all but the ones that are important to them.

These mental filters perform two functions. If you think about how they work for you, as you go about your day-to-day life, you will understand how they work for the people you are trying to reach.

The filters:

1. Block out unwanted messages, of course. Without those filters, our heads would explode as we tried to process not only the

commercial messages we see but all the emails we receive, text messages, and "alerts" that come in through our smartphones, etc.

2. Select what communications we are going to pay attention to, the ones that are most relevant to our lives.

Not surprisingly, as messages have increased in volume—literally, in the case of television ads, but also in terms of the intensity of the rhetoric used in many of the commercial/political/charitable communications out there (our last two elections have shown that heated language has escalated dramatically)—our mental filters have grown stronger. While there are exceptions, of course, as we will see, only messages that help us to create more meaning in our lives are getting through.

Your job, as someone who communicates for a living? To tailor your message so that it passes through these filters.

FILTERS, WHAT FILTERS?

What are these filters that we are talking about? Well, there are a lot of them. Let's start with the ones you'd expect. Ads for supplemental Medicare insurance don't register with teenagers; people in their 60s typically don't pay attention to Red Bull and video game commercial messages aimed at teens and young adults.

But those sorts of filters have always been in place. That's also true about the ones that people use to describe themselves ("risk-taker," "politically conservative/liberal/independent," "spiritual [or not]," "idealistic," "happy," and "compassionate"). And those familiar types of labels can be externally directed as well (for example, "I am someone who cares for family and friends" and/or "I am in a loving relationship").

But what you may not have known is that the people you are trying to reach have filters for dealing with commercial messages and brands aimed specifically at them.

These are the filters that we touched on briefly in Chapter 1. There are eight of them that naturally fall into four quadrants. For your messages to get through, the recipients must feel that those communications meet at least one of the following requirements:

Thinking

- It helps me meet my needs.

- It makes my life easier.

Community

- Being associated with it makes me feel better about myself.

- I want people to know I am associated with it.

Values

- I associate the message/idea with values important to me.

- It stands for the same things I do.

Sensory

- I like the feeling when I'm around it.

- It inspires me.

WHAT THIS MEANS FOR YOU

Let's pause here and underscore something about what this means for organizations in general and your marketing/communication efforts in particular. We will start with the biggest thing to consider—where you must begin your marketing efforts.

You need to go where the consumer already is and reach them on their terms—not yours—to get through their filters.

Both parts of that **bold** sentence are extremely important.

You can't wait for potential customers to find you because they have too many choices, and their filters are locked in place. You may never pop up on their internal radar unless you try to reach them on their own terms, engaging with them by stressing the features, attributes, and feelings associated with your product or service that will get through their thinking, sensory, community, and values filters.

That last point is what's new. You probably already know that you need to reach your customers/audience where they are. (And a lot of them are at home now.) But finding them is not enough. You need to understand the filters they have in place in order to forge a connection.

This means that every part of your communications/ marketing efforts must contain at least one of the factors we talked about before. It must engage with people on a thinking, sensory, community, or values basis.

> If you don't understand the filters your customers—and the people you would like to be your customers—have in place, you are leaving whether your message gets through to chance. Hoping to get lucky doesn't strike us as a sound business strategy.

That is, of course, not what most of us do.

While we talk a good game about how our communications and marketing messages must be all about the customer, even a cursory glance shows we often fall short.

For example, it is lovely that some car companies boast about how their vehicles can go 500 miles on a tank of gas, with the implicit message being that drivers will have to stop at the gas pump less often. Still, those communications—whether they are in a commercial, print ad, or online—could make that benefit much more consumer-centric, breaking through the consumers' filters in the process.

The car companies could, for instance, show a harried work-at-home parent with a long "to-do" list sitting on the dashboard of their car, impatiently drumming their fingers while waiting for their gas tank to fill with the voice-over being "don't you have enough to do without having to stop for gas? Well, the XYZ-mobile goes 517 miles between fill-ups." Positioning the message this way would get through the thinking filters ("Hey, they are talking about making life easier.") And maybe even the values filters as well ("I want to be perceived as someone who always uses their time efficiently.")

As a rule, marketers are better than communicators in crafting messages that have a chance to get through our audience's filters. But as we just saw with that fictional car ad, even they could do much better. Far too often, we all send out messages that simply don't register with the people we are trying to reach. There may be nothing inherently bad in these communications. But benign is not enough today. Our messages need to resonate, and there is no chance of that happening if they cannot get past the filters that our target audience has in place.

RELEVANCE

DO YOU KNOW WHO YOU ARE
TRYING TO REACH?

One reason we don't do a better job attaching our marketing message to the relevance filters our customers use is that we simply don't know enough about our customers to do that.

Here's a simple, real-world example.

An upscale department store noticed one of their male credit cardholders bought a new expensive suit. As a result, the guy started getting ads on a regular basis telling him what other clothing was being featured, and he received various inducements to get him to buy.

It was also clear that the department store had sold his name to other retailers, so he started receiving fashion-related messages from those stores as well.

Nothing surprising here. This happens all the time.

But the guy was like most men. He didn't buy clothes all that often, so all the communication was wasted, along with a huge opportunity that marketers didn't know about.

You see, the man had bought the new expensive suit to wear at his first-born's wedding. Had marketers known that, they could have made all kinds of appealing offers. ("A major change in your life? Terrific. Now is a great time to check in with a new financial services company [lawyer, accountant]." Or, "Hey, is there a new addition to your family? Great. Get them off on the right foot with…")

The department store, for example, could have sent him a 20 percent off coupon for buying the happy couple a wedding gift, and the store could have offered to make his son and his new daughter-in-law credit card customers (giving them a "welcome new customers" discount as well).

All this would have been possible if the department store just understood why the guy, who had never bought clothing from the store before, purchased a new, expensive suit.

The purpose of this book isn't to tell you how to take advantage of the data (and as you will see, we are big fans of big data) that would allow you to conclude that the man was buying the suit for his son's wedding.

Instead, our point here is that the more you truly know about people you are trying to reach, the easier it is to create messages for them that will actually get through.

Clothing ads had no meaning to this man. It was simply something he didn't think about. But the importance of family? That was a completely other matter—and an opportunity that countless marketers missed.

We will be talking more about how you can identify the exact people you are trying to reach in the second half of the book.

It is rare to find a leader or marketer who understands these filters and uses them effectively all the time. Why? They simply don't think about their customers this way. We continue to look for a woman 18-49 or someone over 65 who has a certain household income. That approach can work to some extent because it has always worked to some extent. But it is remarkably inefficient if you don't tailor it more precisely.

Let's take a real example. Let's say you are in the media business. You publish a mass-market magazine or own a cable news channel. You certainly could market as you always did—or you can add our filters to the mix.

If you did, you would discover, as we did through our research, that Millennials and people 65 and older are most loyal to their media sources. Those two cohorts scored highest when we asked questions involving the thinking filter ("it helps me meet my needs," "it makes my life easier") and the values filter ("I associate the message/idea with values important to me," "it stands for the same things I do") associated with media properties.

RELEVANCE

A RELEVANCE MOMENT

Relevance can be formed in a moment.

Literally.

Two quick examples—one shocking, one sweet.

One of your two authors (Paul) can vividly remember the moment he decided he would never smoke. He was nine.

It happened during a commercial break in the baseball game he was watching. The station announcer said they were about to run an anti-smoking public service announcement (PSA). No big deal. This happened all the time, and even someone who was not yet 10 knew he would be bored by the message that would follow.

But this spot was different. It opened with a close-up on an old black and white photo of what even someone who was not yet interested in girls knew was a stunningly gorgeous young lady. The camera then cut to someone who was about the same age as the boy's mom. But her grey hair and wrinkled face made her look far older.

The woman was in a hospital bed, holding what he later learned was called a tracheostomy microphone to the middle of her throat.

In a distorted, eerie voice—the result of using the trachea microphone—she said, referring to the black and white photo, "that was me before smoking took my looks and my voice."

"This is me today."

It was clear that the now wizened woman had to breathe through a hole in her throat and would be talking with that distorted, electronically enhanced voice forever. It was the scariest thing the boy had ever seen. When he got older, he never once seriously thought about smoking. The image of that woman talking directly to the camera (and to him) made sure of that.

The anti-smoking spot had made it through all four quadrants, as we can see by going through the checklist.

Thinking? There was no way the boy wanted to end up like that woman. He would make a conscious decision not to smoke.

Social? Sure, some people thought smoking was cool. But who would want to be associated with a group of people who didn't understand its potentially devastating impact?

Values? This one hit home the hardest. The nine-year-old boy pictured himself as playing third base for the N.Y. Yankees in his future. Smoking could make sure that NEVER happened.

Sensory? Another solid hit. The message inspired him to swear off cigarettes before he could ever start.

A shocking (and sad) message had gotten through.

ON A MORE POSITIVE NOTE

On the other hand, Gillette, the shaving company, has created the Treo, the first razor designed for caregivers.

When the product, now available everywhere, was in its trial stage, samples were given to professional caregivers and anyone else who wanted one, so the company could gain feedback and make refinements. The demand was such that the company ran out of samples.

That shouldn't have been surprising. According to the American Society of Aging, "over 8 million older adults in the U.S. annually receive assistance with activities of daily living—including shaving—from family or professional caregivers, and over 34.2 million Americans have provided basic care to adults 50 years or older in the past year."

In fact, Google statistics show that tens of thousands of conversations happen about the demands of everyday caregiving. "Inspired by real-world conversations just like these, Gillette began its journey of developing and researching a product to address this very emotional consumer need," said Melissa Monich, vice president of research and development, global grooming at P&G,

[Continued]

which owns Gillette.

During its research, Gillette discovered a surprising fact: "Based on U.S. patent filings, over 4,000 razors have been designed for the purpose of shaving yourself, but zero have been specifically engineered for shaving another person."

"We were struck by how important day-to-day activities (like shaving) are in supporting the dignity, pride, and morale of those who need assistance," Monich said. "This made us even more compelled to use our expertise to develop a more comfortable and safer experience."

It also made Gillette (more) relevant to lots of people. It is suddenly not just another company that makes razors and razor blades. It was the only (as we write this) company making a razor designed for caregivers.

Think about the challenge for a minute. The new razor had to be designed to meet the needs of not one person but two: the caregiver and the individual getting the shave.

The fact that the company took on the challenge helped it forge a closer connection to its customers in general and the people who need the new razor in particular.

Just like the anti-smoking ad, the messages about the Treo had broken through the filters.

CREATING A MOMENT

As both stories show, creating a moment can be powerful. It can get people to see your brand or cause in a new light, make them more receptive to what you have to say, and influence their behavior. The moment gets their attention, and once you have their attention, you can introduce a new idea.

The question is, how do you create a moment?

Sometimes, they simply occur by chance. A person driving through the South stopped to buy a brand of gas that he usually doesn't purchase. It was about a month after devastating hurricanes had hit the region. While he was filling in his tank, he noticed a banner hanging over the pumps saying: "For the next three months, a portion of your purchase will be donated to those whose homes were destroyed in our region. We are committed to giving $8 million."

Suddenly, that unfamiliar kind of gasoline has become more relevant to the person buying gas; he knew people who had lost their homes.

But you can't count on serendipity to create a relevant moment. Are there specific steps you can take? Yes, let us give you three.

Surprise. The PSA spot is a perfect example. It wasn't just another "stop smoking ad" or yet another boring message about why you shouldn't start. At the time, it was a striking, unusual, and extremely effective way of making the point that smoking can ruin your life.

Delight. We love it when companies, brands, or even elected officials take on an issue or problem that is important to us.

Make them do a double-take. A maker of prescription opioids takes out full-page ads saying they want to be part of the solution to the epidemic; an extremely rich person like Warren Buffett saying his taxes are too low. That's the sort of thing we are talking about here. Once you get someone to look at you in a new light, it is easier to forge a connection.

It only takes a moment.

What can you do with that information? A lot. For one thing, it will allow you to make more informed decisions about where you spend your marketing budget. Do you target Millennials and Boomers because you know they are loyal to your brand and you always want to strengthen your core, or do you do the minimum there—since they are so loyal—and use your marketing dollars to try to attract new customers?

No matter which route you choose, you can go to the people who advertise and point out how strong you are with Millennials and Boomers and suggest that clients trying to reach either of those two groups should spend their money with you.

OKAY, BUT WHY THESE FILTERS?

Right about this time, we have usually convinced people that their customers—and the people they would like to be their customers—have filters in place, and they need to take that into account when crafting marketing, communication, and advocacy messages of all kinds.

But invariably, they ask: Why these four quadrants? Why is it thinking, sensory, values, and community as opposed to something else? Couldn't there be more than the four general categories that you've named?

Let's start with the second question first. Of course, there could have been more and/or other filters.

When we were first starting to compile all the ways people decide to pay attention to a message—or decide not to—we came up with 50 potential filters. For example, we considered such things as "habits" because if you have always bought a certain brand of coffee, or type of car (domestic, import), it is very difficult for someone to get you to switch. That buying filter is well-entrenched.

Economic relevance could have had its own category, instead of being part of the thinking quadrant, because money is such a big part of our lives. Then there was the question of time, or more specifically temporal relevance, which clearly could have been a quadrant. What is important to you when you are a teenager may no longer be relevant to you when you are sixty-two. Conversely, what is important to you once you retire—access to the best hospitals and doctors, perhaps—may not have any relevance to you in your thirties when health problems were not so prevalent.

And we endlessly debated whether to give emotion its own quadrant.

But the reason we didn't include emotion will actually help you see why we settled on the four categories we did.

Emotion cuts a wide path, appearing in three of the four quadrants we ultimately decided to use. Clearly, our senses trigger emotion, so does community (you love your family), and values (you believe cancer should be eradicated, so you give to the American Cancer Society). We could have separated emotion instead of including it as a subset of something else, but we were confident it was covered by the filters we settled on.

Similarly, habit might have had its own quadrant instead of being subsumed into thinking and sensory appeal.

BUT WE COULD HAVE TAKEN A DIFFERENT ROUTE

But of course, we could have sliced and diced the information differently, using psychologist Abraham Maslow's well-known hierarchy of needs (following), for example.

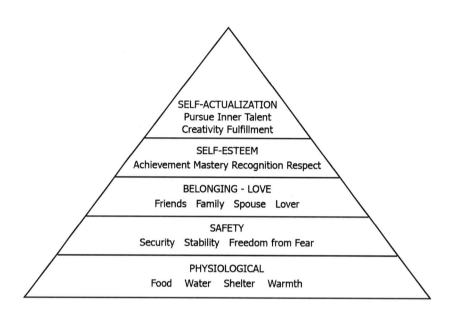

Similarly, we could have taken the psychographic approach used by the VALS (values, attitudes, and lifestyles) system and put the customers we are trying to reach in categories such as innovators, thinkers, experiencers, etc., and decided to label the filters that way. (We will talk about these alternative approaches in the next chapter.)

> The filters we all have in place always let through insights that trigger meaning in our lives.

But even if we had used one of these other methodologies, we would have ended up with a list of quadrants remarkably similar to what we have. We were aiming for a framework that would help us understand how people attach themselves to ideas, causes, actions, and things. We were not trying to segment people. We were trying to understand and segment the relationship *people* have to *things*—ideas, experiences, purchases, and the like. It is a subtle but important difference.

Is this the only way you can think about filters? And is ours the only set of filters you can use? Of course not. If you want to create your own, we are all for it. The important thing is for you to recognize the filters—no matter which ones you use—are there.

With that by way of background, let's look at our four general quadrants in more detail.

THE FILTERS THEMSELVES

Thinking. This is the filter that covers most of what goes on in the "left" (or logical) part of your brain.

It is functional. It's concerned with the specifications of a product, such as where you can find it, its price, and the features it has. "I am looking for an inexpensive, dependable car. Hmmm. The ads for the Nissan Versa and Honda Civic check those boxes. Let me pay attention to what they are telling me."

Community. It's all about the relationships your audience has and the ones they would like to have. Part and parcel of that is how the world perceives your target customer and how they would like to be perceived. Community includes such things as the groups people belong to and who they hang out with at work and outside of it. It also includes their online and offline communities or tribes. (We will be discussing tribes in detail in the next chapter.)

Values. These are the ethical, moral, and faith-based elements that connect you with ideas outside of yourself. This may include your place of worship, the way you see the world (whether you believe people are basically good or evil, and whether they deserve the lives they get or have their lives determined by factors outside their control). It can be as simple as a statement of what you believe—to as complex as the way you view humankind's destiny.

Sensory. The retail and hospitality folks get this one. This category includes everything you see, touch, smell, and hear as part of an interaction. Think of what music is playing as you enter a hotel lobby or how the merchandise is displayed in your favorite boutique. That new car smell is a classic example of effective sensory appeal. How an iPhone feels in your hand is part of it as well. Sensory appeal also includes such things as comfort, safety, and routine. As we will see, this is a significantly underestimated category.

WHAT'S WRONG WITH WHAT I AM DOING?

Do these filters need to replace the ways you have been segmenting the market?

Well, in the best of all worlds, they could work in conjunction with them.

If you are happy with the way you are currently approaching the market, the filters can, indeed, function as an add-on, and you can use them during any part of the marketing process. They can help you formulate a strategy when you are first starting out. They can help you fine-tune what you have when you are underway and help you decide where you will go next. They are also extremely useful when you are trying to solve marketing challenges.

But ask yourself this:

• Is my business growing?

• Am I getting new customers?

• Are my customers brand-loyal?

• Do people perceive my company (product, service) as exciting and innovative?

If the answer to even one of these questions is no—then it may be time to replace the way you segment the market.

Does this mean every communication/marketing effort must touch on all four of the quadrants?

No. But they need to touch at least one, at the minimum, and if you want it to be effective, you want to make sure that two of the quadrants are really strong.

DON'T LET DATA WAG THE INSIGHT DOG

As long as we are pointing out things to watch out for and problems to avoid, let us add one more.

We love analytics and are big believers in big data. Who wouldn't like all the research that is right at our fingertips and a relatively easy way to confirm that we are on the right track?

But it is that last phrase that is important. The data can tell you if your insight resonates with customers or if it doesn't, **but it will not be the source of the insight itself.**

The analogy we would draw is to a more primitive type of research—focus groups.

When they first started to come into vogue following World War II, many marketers believed this tool would be the answer to all their prayers. They could have their customers tell them exactly what they wanted. And then, the marketer could create that product or service. It didn't work out that way.

Think back to the 1960s, a time when most people had not been exposed to fast food restaurants because there were relatively few. (McDonald's, which started in California, didn't open its first restaurant east of the Mississippi River until 1955. And that one was in Illinois.) If you asked people where they would like to buy a hamburger, they would have described a better Howard Johnson's or a restaurant that would serve a better hamburger. They wouldn't describe McDonald's because McDonald's—or what we now think

RELEVANCE

of as McDonald's—was beyond their frame of reference.

Our point?

Data can confirm what people want in restaurants (or anything else), but it won't, on its own, lead you to a big idea. We need the creativity of people for that; people who understand what the data is telling us.

TAKEAWAYS FROM CHAPTER 3

1. **Your target market is two steps ahead of you.** While you are trying to figure out how to get your message heard, given all the noise out there—noise that seems to get louder by the day—the time-pressured, over-messaged people you want to reach have already put filters in place to make it even more difficult to reach them.

2. **You need to make sure your message is heard** by having it get past those filters. That means you need to know what those filters are and what it will take to bypass them.

3. **The easiest way to get past those filters?** You need to make sure you are promising to make your audience's life better in some meaningful way—a promise that has been created specifically for them.

4. **Tailoring your message to get past these filters** is more than possible by augmenting the marketing/communications strategies and tactics you have in place. (Or if you are unhappy with your current results, concentrating on getting through the filters could replace what you are doing now.)

4

Clusters of Relevance: A New Way to Segment Your Audience

When you boil everything down, marketing is pretty simple: You figure out who you want to sell to and then determine how you will get them to buy.

In this chapter, we are going to argue that if you want to market successfully going forward—given the uncertainty of the moment, the competition you face, and the challenges of getting through all the filters your customers have in place—you will need to rethink both parts of that sentence.

Let's begin with where we focused our attention in our previous book "Relevance: The Power to Change Minds and Behavior and Stay Ahead of the Competition," on *how you are going to get people to buy (or accept your position)?* As we described there—and summarized in the last chapter—you will only get them to do that by being relevant.

How? You start by figuring out ways to get past the filters the people you are trying to reach have in place. Then, in addition to all the marketing techniques you are currently using, it means searching for clusters of relevance (see sidebar, "But This is Messy!").

SO, WHAT EXACTLY IS A CLUSTER OF RELEVANCE?

Let's create a definition of what we are talking about so that we all start on the same page.

A cluster of relevance is a group of varied people, i.e., those not identified by a common demographic group (women 18-34,

RELEVANCE

Hispanics over the age of 50), who come together for a common purpose or experience.

You can find examples everywhere. There are people of all ages, ethnicities, and backgrounds who choose to stay only at "green hotels." And look at the people who own all those Great Danes who gather every Sunday at the park or who are passionate S.F. Giants baseball fans. If you look around Oracle Park during a Giants home game, you would be hard-pressed to find what those 40,000 people have in common, other than the activity that brings them together (in this case, rooting for the Giants while having a great time at what could be the most fan-friendly ballpark in America). You can instantly see how marketing clusters tie into what we talked about in the first two chapters.

Remember we said consumers have filters in place that block all but the messages that they find most relevant.

Relevance cluster: a group of varied people united solely by common purpose or experience.

By identifying a relevance cluster, you are instantly going to break through those filters. For example, there are people who obsess about coffee. It could be Dunkin', Starbucks, or a regional brand like Red Diamond in the South, but they can't imagine going through the day without having a cup (or three). Coffee gets through the sensory filter, of course, and quite possibly the thinking filter as well, the one where people ask, "does this help me meet my needs?"

Conversely (and somewhat surprisingly to many), there can be a cluster of relevance among people who hate coffee. Garth Brooks won't drink coffee. He prefers hot chocolate, and football's Bill Belichick absolutely can't stand it, going so far as to refuse anything coffee-flavored.

Similarly, all types of people believe in sustainability, the idea that all the resources to produce something should be continuously replaced so that we don't deplete the earth. Sustainability appeals to the social filter about how we see ourselves and how we want others to see us. ("It makes me feel better about myself," and "I want people to know I am associated with it.")

OFFENSE/DEFENSE

So far, so good. But why do you need to fold clusters of relevance into your marketing program?

There are two reasons—and they both involve increasing your revenues and profits.

"BUT THIS IS MESSY!"

Invariably, one of the pushbacks we get when we start talking about marketing clusters is, "but this is messy. You mean that I have to deal with the fact that both women in their 20s, and those in their late 60s, are passionate about their belief that animals, in whatever environment, need to be treated ethically and humanely, and I need to figure a way to reach both groups?"

Well, in a word, yes.

Marketing clusters are not as neat and tidy as dividing your customers into segments like "Black women over 55." But the fact of the matter is people are messy. They don't easily fit into little boxes that say "all men over 60 are X," and quite frankly, people get resentful when we try to put them in little boxes. (Doubt us? Ask yourself how you feel when a marketer does it to you.)

[Continued]

RELEVANCE

We are not advocating that you throw away all the traditional segmentation techniques that divide people neatly. We are just saying that you want to add marketing clusters to the mix to get more people to engage with your product, service, or idea.

For one thing, thinking about the clusters will help you get new customers. As you find new linkages between your customers' interests—biking, for example—and your product, you find new ways to reach people who might be interested in your product whom you never considered targeting before.

It allows you to be proactive and go after that group.

On the other hand, it also serves as a defensive measure. If you find more things that interest your customers, you will have more ways to appeal to them.

Let's say you sell hardwood floors and people really like them. The fact that you decide to add sustainable woods deepens the relationship you have with the segment of those people who find that aspect important.

In short, you are adding the idea of marketing clusters to your attempt to reach customers to do three things:

1. **Retain your current customers.** You always want to be relevant to them; showing you share their commitment to sustainability when it comes to flooring, does that.

2. **Get more sales from your current customers.** By broadening your product line, you may entice someone to start that remodeling project they have been thinking about.

3. **Broaden your base.** Expand your reach to drive behavior change and attract new customers.

The upshot of all of the above is that it will allow your ideas to scale and lead to (hopefully) wide-scale behavioral change.

WHY DATA ALONE WON'T SAVE US

When we start talking about relevance clusters, it doesn't take long for someone to wonder if finding them can be done automatically. They ask: "Won't all the advanced analytics we have and are developing uncover all the linkages I am currently missing and tweak whatever flaws I have in my current approach to finding clusters?"

While we mentioned in the last chapter that we are huge fans of analytics, the answer is no. You will never be able to find the linkages with just computers alone. As you search for relevance clusters, what is needed is really smart software and really smart people who know how to use it (i.e., a combination of computers and creatives). You need shrewd, clever people to use all the technological tools we have access to.

But that has always been the case, as Walter Isaacson, who wrote the celebrated biographies of Steve Jobs and Albert Einstein, points out in "The Innovators: How a Group of Inventors, Hackers, Geniuses, and Geeks Created the Digital Revolution."

"The most creative innovations of the digital age came from those who were able to connect the arts and sciences," he writes. "They believed that beauty mattered. 'I always thought of myself as a humanities person as a kid, but I liked electronics,' Steve Jobs told me when I embarked on his biography. 'Then I read something that one of my heroes, Edwin Land of Polaroid, said about the importance of people who could stand at the intersection of humanities and sciences, and I decided that's what I wanted to do.' The people who were comfortable at this humanities-technology intersection helped to create the human-machine symbiosis that is at the core of this story."

As Isaacson is quick to add, the "idea that innovation resides where art and science connect is not new." Leonardo da Vinci was the poster boy, of course, "and his drawing of the Vitruvian

[Continued]

RELEVANCE

Man became the symbol, of the creativity that flourishes when the humanities and sciences interact."

THE VITRUVIAN MAN

As the BBC said in a special about da Vinci: "This sketch, and the notes that go with it, shows how Leonardo understood the proportions of the human body. Each separate part was a simple fraction of the whole."

For example, the head measured from the forehead to the chin was exactly one-tenth of the total height, and the outstretched arms were always as wide as the body was tall.

"These ideas were not Leonardo's but were taken from the writings of the Roman architect Vitruvius. Both men believed that the same principles should be used when designing buildings." When Einstein got stymied while working out General Relativity, he would pull out his violin and play Mozart until he could reconnect to what he called the "harmony of the spheres."

"We humans can remain relevant in an era of cognitive computing because we are able to think differently, something that an algorithm, almost by definition, can't master. We possess an imagination that, as English mathematician Ada Lovelace, the woman who has been called 'the first computer programmer' for writing an algorithm for a 'computing machine' that was built in the 1800s, said, 'brings together things, facts, ideas, conceptions in new, original, endless, ever-varying combinations.'

"We discern patterns and appreciate their beauty. We weave information into narratives."

IT'S SURPRISING WHAT YOU'LL FIND

Here's an example of the sort of thing we are talking about when it comes to clusters of relevance.

Picture an Audi driver. What comes to mind, and what kind of music do they listen to? And more importantly, how would you position your marketing and communication messages to appeal to them if you are selling something other than a car?

If you are like most people, you said the driver is "male," and because you may have a picture of a graying Baby Boomer in mind—putting him in his 50s, let's say—you might have said that he really likes listening to "classic rock," or the '80s channel on Sirius-XM.

Well, it turns out that the typical Audi buyer is younger than those who buy other luxury brands, and Audi has a far larger percentage of female drivers than you might think.

RELEVANCE

Okay, you probably could have found that out through traditional research techniques. But if you are looking for clusters of relevance, you would find a semi-surprising thing when you began talking to those younger, female drivers. A significant percentage of them listen to country music.

But again, maybe that would not be surprising (if you are constantly searching for unusual connections). On average, country music is one of the favored formats among people 18-54, and 54 percent of the listeners to country stations are female. So, the gross numbers alone would say the people at the upper end of the 18-54 range are likely to be female.

But country music fans driving Audis? Really? The stereotype would be an inexpensive truck, right?

Well, no. The average listener to a country station has a family income 50 percent higher than the national average, and one-third of those households—34 percent to be precise—earn more than $100,000 a year, according to figures compiled by the Country Music Association.

The takeaway: Through a combination of traditional segmentation techniques—age, income—and out-of-the-box probing to find interesting linkages—you have discovered a significant number of well-heeled Audi drivers listen to country music.

Okay, all this is interesting, you say, but so what?

Well, suppose you are Target, a department store chain that prides itself on appealing to women with more money than most. (Target has a higher percentage of female shoppers than Kohl's and Walmart, according to Ad Age, and about a third of them have a household income of $75,000 or greater.)

If you are Target, what do you do if you know that a surprisingly high percentage of female shoppers are country music fans? Well, you expand the selection of CDs you offer, of course, and maybe put the latest CD from Miranda Lambert or Brad Paisley near the shoe section. But you also start running (even more) commercials during the Country Music Awards.

Less obviously, you begin to run ads on country music stations in the top five markets in the country (those markets are, in order, New York, Los Angeles, Chicago, Philadelphia, and Dallas-Fort Worth. Surprised?)—where one in four people listening to the radio is a country fan—and you start thinking about redesigning your stores. Why? Because it turns out that country music fans spend a disproportionate amount of their time entertaining family and friends at home. So, you would think about expanding your home décor department to take advantage of that fact.

By doing all this, you grow closer to a key market for you; country music fans who might have been shopping at Kohl's and Walmart, and you might attract even more high-end shoppers.

You need to know where the marketing clusters are so you can tap into them. If you do, you remain relevant to your customers who have more choices than ever before. The whole purpose of this exercise is to drive behavioral change (and keep the customers you have.)

THIS IS AN ADD-ON

Let's stop here and make explicit something we have mentioned in passing throughout. The idea of searching for marketing clusters is designed to work *with* your current marketing efforts. It does not replace them; it represents an additional part of your customer analysis, and that word "analysis" is important.

The rise of "big data" and analytics has been wonderful. We now have all kinds of information about our customers and that, of course, lets us serve them better. But as we start to employ that data more and more in everything we do, many of us have lost sight of the fact—and it is a fact—that not every insight into our customers can be found through analytics, as we have stressed throughout. Worse, there is a natural tendency to use data to reinforce our biases.

The idea of confirmation bias, the tendency to search for, interpret, favor, and recall information in a way that confirms one's preexisting beliefs or hypotheses, is far from new, and you see it all the time. If you believe that all left-handed people are extremely creative, you will easily recall the left-handed people who were, conveniently forgetting all the southpaws who weren't. Perhaps the clearest example of people searching out confirmation for their beliefs can be found on television. Think of the people who watch Fox News and those who prefer MSNBC, and what their political inclinations are.

The use of marketing clusters helps us to take a fresh—and complementary—look at not only the data but at our customers themselves. But to use it effectively means you need to be open to looking at data and your customers in new ways.

Some will suggest we have always segmented people along traditional lines as a way of pushing back on this approach.

True. But things change. On a macro level, just think about how different the world is in the 21st century. We are connected globally; brands have begun positioning themselves not only to be market leaders at home but around the world, and the way people are interacting with what we have to sell is changing as well. (When was the last time someone called from a landline and asked to be mailed a printed brochure?)

To see what all this change means on a micro level, take a look at the financial services industry. For literally decades, they have made marketing to Baby Boomers their number one priority. But the oldest Baby Boomer is now over 70, and the youngest is well over 50. The industry needs to focus on the next generation and the generation after that (the Baby Boomers' grandchildren. Yikes!)

In this kind of environment, our smartest clients have started looking for patterns of behaviors that cross all cohorts. We need to do it, too. And that's where clusters of relevance can help enormously. Traditional techniques miss the linkages.

THE PARTY OF THE FIRST PART

Remember where we began this discussion. We said marketing at its essence is nothing more than figuring out who you want to sell to and then determining how you are going to get them to buy. Our discussion of relevance and relevance clusters takes care of the second part of that definition, how you are going to get people to buy. Now let's look at the first part and see how we can figure out how we want to target.

Typically, you determine that by sorting people quantitatively using various segmentation techniques. You might start with gender. For example, you say, "I am going to sell to women," "I am going to sell to men," or "I am going to sell to both men and women."

For the sake of this discussion, let's say you have decided your primary audience is men. From there, you would segment further quantitatively. (I am going to sell to men age 25-49 who have an annual household income greater than $75,000.)

This is traditionally the kind of segmentation that we do as marketers, and the problem with it is obvious and twofold. Let's use a very specific example to show why.

To pick a situation at random, let's say your target audience is women 18-34 who have a household income of less than $50,000 a year. Within that demo, you have: female college and graduate students; women who stopped their formal education after senior year in high school and married early and have two or more children that they are raising at home; young women—some of whom are college graduates, some who are not—who are just getting their careers underway; women who have decided to leave the workforce for a while to have their first child, etc.

You get the idea. It is hard to find a common denominator, especially once you factor in that some of the women live on farms and rural areas, others in big cities like Chicago, Los Angeles, or New York, and the rest in the suburbs. The fact is that two 26-year-old women—the midpoint of your demo—can be extremely different, and a one-size-fits-all approach is not going to work if you are trying to get them to pay attention to what you have to say or sell. A message that resonates with one may not resonate with the other.

That's bad. But what is even worse is that since most of your competitors are marketing to the exact same group—women age 18-34 in this case—competition is going to be fierce.

One thing that would help a lot is to find other women you could appeal to, women who like your product but who are not in what you think is your core demo. And that is where the concept of relevance clusters comes back in. For example, it turns out that, for whatever reason, women who are extreme cyclists—meaning they pedal more than 50 miles at a time—are fond of your product. This includes women 18-34, but it also includes teens who are a bit younger, as well as women in their 40s, 50s, and 60s and, in some cases, older.

No, you are not going to totally upend your marketing and target extreme cyclists exclusively. But they could represent a nice bump in your sales if you go after them in addition to your core market. (And if you probe a bit further, you might discover that women who identify themselves as "animal lovers" are extremely fond of your product as well. That represents another potential increase in sales and earnings for you.)

If you don't know what the people who like your product have in common, beyond the obvious ("we know we appeal to women 18-34"), you lose on two grounds:

1. You miss out on a chance to increase sales beyond your core group.
2. You are doomed to compete head-to-head where the competition is most fierce. (All your competitors are targeting women 18-34 as well.)

> If you market the way you always have, you are going to miss a huge number of opportunities.

One way to get around this problem, some marketers will tell you, is to use different segmentation techniques such as VALS or Myers-Briggs. It is an intriguing thought, and we are all for having more arrows in your marketing and communications quiver, but both VALS and Myers-Briggs are flawed as well.

To see why, let's start with VALS, which was created by Strategic Business Insights. When it was first used in the late 1970s, it was based on social values, and the name was an acronym for Values and Lifestyles. However, currently, as the company writes on its website, "VALS is based on selected psychological traits and key demographics instead of values, so we dropped 'values and lifestyles' but retained the VALS brand."

What VALs does is characterize people by personality types. You answer questions about yourself such as "I am often interested in theories;" "I like to lead others" by picking one of four choices: "mostly disagree;" "somewhat disagree;" "somewhat agree;" "mostly agree." And then, based on your responses, you are sorted into one of eight categories.

The categories and what they mean according to VALS:

Innovators: "sophisticated, in charge, curious."

Thinkers: "informed, reflective, content."

Believers: "literal, loyal, moralistic."

Achievers: "self-focused, conventional, status-seekers."

Strivers: "insecure, imitative, undisciplined."

Experiencers: "trendsetting, impulsive, variety-seeking."

Makers: "responsible, practical, self-sufficient."

Survivors: "nostalgic, cautious, trusting."

It is an intriguing approach, and it is indeed helpful to know that if someone is an "innovator," they are "active consumers and their purchases reflect cultivated tastes of upscale, niche products and services," and that "although their incomes allow them many choices, 'thinkers' are conservative, practical consumers; they look for durability, functionality, and value in the products they buy."

But implicit in this sort of characterization is that all "innovators" or all "thinkers" are the same, and so we are back to the one-size-fits-all problem, i.e., all women 18-34 are the same, something that Myers-Briggs is guilty of as well.

The Myers-Briggs Type Indicator (MBTI) groups people into one of 16 categories based on how they answer various questions given an "agree" or "disagree" choice. ("You are rather impatient.

Agree? Disagree?" "A logical decision is always best whether or not it hurts someone's feelings. Agree? Disagree?") There is no middle ground when it comes to these questions. You must either agree or disagree.

The four letters that make up your type can help you understand yourself and your interactions with others and would seem on the surface to be a perfect way to segment people.

Each personality type in Myers-Briggs is explained by four letters in combination. Here is what the letters mean, according to the organization's website.

E = Extraversion. You have "the need to talk things through. Keywords: Outgoing. Talkative. Sociable."

F = Feeling. You "consider others before making decisions. Keywords: Compassionate. Personal. Warm."

I = Introversion. You have "the need to think things through. Keywords: Shy. Reserved. Reflective."

J = Judging. You "love routine and to-do lists. Keywords: Scheduled. Structured. Organized."

N = Intuition. You "can see the big picture and future possibilities. Keywords: Brainstormer. Theory."

P = Perceiving. You are someone who "enjoys surprises and changing plans. Keywords: Go-with-the-flow. Unscheduled. Flexible."

S = Sensing. You "trust the establishment and the tried and true. Keywords: Facts. Details. Data Collection."

T = Thinking. You "use the logical choice. Keywords: Rational. Black and white. Tough-minded."

RELEVANCE

And it is lovely that someone who is an "ISTJ" can be described, as Myers-Briggs does, as "quiet, serious, earns success by thoroughness and dependability. Practical, matter-of-fact, realistic, and responsible. Decides logically what should be done and works toward it steadily, regardless of distractions. Takes pleasure in making everything orderly and organized—their work, their home, their life. Values traditions and loyalty."

And on the same level, it is helpful to know that an "ESTP" is "flexible and tolerant, they take a pragmatic approach focused on immediate results. Theories and conceptual explanations bore them— they want to act energetically to solve the problem. Their focus is on the here and now; they're spontaneous; they enjoy each moment that they can be active with others. Enjoy material comforts and style. Learn best through doing."

Each of those descriptions gives you a good idea about how you should market to, and communicate with, these types of people.

But again, this approach to classifying people assumes that everyone who falls into one of Myers-Briggs' 16 categories is basically the same, i.e., it assumes one ESTP is just like another. Like VALs, Myers-Briggs puts everyone who responds the same way in a bucket, and as a result, marketers and communicators implicitly think everyone in that bucket is interchangeable.

We can't help but draw the analogy to astrology and the 12 signs of the Zodiac. Is it really true that 1/12th of the population—men and women—are identical, based on the month they were born in? That every Leo or Cancer or Capricorn is basically the same?

The problem with classifying people this way was put perfectly by Isabel Briggs Myers, the co-creator (with her mother) of the Myers-Briggs assessment, who said, "it is up to each person to recognize his or her true preferences."

We would substitute the word "marketer" for "person" in that sentence.

We need to recognize the unique preferences of our customers and understand that one person who is a Myers-Briggs' "T," or thinker, could prefer Sony televisions, while another "T," using the same logical and tough-minded decision process, could walk out of the store with an LG.

> VALS and Myers-Briggs are wonderful tools. But—and it is a big but—nothing is as black and white as they make it seem.

Since that is the case, we need a new way to think about how to find our customers—and that is exactly where the idea of marketing clusters fits in. Instead of assuming everyone who on the surface seems to be the same—women 18-34, VALS's strivers, or a Myers-Briggs' INFPs—it starts with the assumption that there might be some similarities between people who, at first glance, may not have a lot in common.

In other words, it creates a web that links various people instead of placing them into individual buckets. With this approach, there are fewer boundaries around the people you are trying to reach; it helps you cast a wider—but still concentrated—net.

RELEVANCE

1. **If you market the way everyone else does,** you will never have a competitive advantage. At best, all you will do is reach a tie against the people you are battling with.

2. **There are even more problems with matching the competition.** For one thing, it assumes that they have figured out a way to capture every opportunity out there. (Odds are they haven't.) In addition, while you stop to study the competition, they are continuing to improve, causing you to fall further behind.

3. **The net result of points 1 + 2: You need to add more unique tools** as you try to figure out how to break through all the filters your customers and potential customers have in place. That is why you want to be relevant.

4. **Searching for marketing clusters,** groups of varied people united solely by a common purpose or experience can help you both find new customers. It can also bring you closer to the ones you already have.

5

Connecting With Your Customers by Understanding the Tribes They Belong To

In this chapter, we are going to build off of the concept of "relevance clusters" that we discussed in the last one.

When a cluster of people form close ties to one another, the resulting group can be described as a tribe. And as we will explain, if you understand the tribes people belong to—not only the customary ones like family, social groups, community, and traditions, but also affinity groups, friends, and shared experiences—you'll have a significant advantage when it comes to marketing to your customers and the people you would like to be your customers.

Tribes increase the importance of relevance through their shared experiences and interests.

> "For millions of years, human beings have been part of one tribe or another. A group needs only two things to be a tribe: a shared interest and a way to communicate."
>
> --*Seth Godin in his book "Tribes: We Need You to Lead Us"*

The concept of "tribes" is, at the same time, both an ancient and modern idea. It is, perhaps, one of the most basic and enduring organizing concepts behind human behavior and human history. People cluster and organize around what they have in common: ancestry, community, faith, or custom, for example.

RELEVANCE

But today, the concept of "tribe" goes far beyond that to include shared experiences, views, and tastes.

People who served in the Navy are members of a tribe, of course. But it is reasonable to assume that sub-groups inside the Navy, like Navy Seals, have an even stronger tribal relationship. Women alumnae could be the basis for a tribe. But female graduates of small, all-women's colleges—schools like Simmons, Spelman, or Stephens—are likely to have stronger ties to each other than most college graduates.

Tribes can be permanent, as the examples above show. Once a Navy Seal, always a Navy Seal; you are an alumna of a women's college forever. But modern-day tribes can also be temporary and transitory. They can develop, shift, morph, assemble, and disassemble in real time. They emerge in reaction and response to changing social, economic, and cultural trends.

Need an example? Just look at the recent U.S. Presidential elections. During the campaigns in 2016 and 2020, unlikely people got together to form tribes to elect Donald Trump originally or to make sure he wasn't re-elected later on.

None of this has been lost on marketers and communicators. We have long tailored campaigns to identifiable and reachable segments of people. But in the past, we tended to focus on tribal affiliations that stemmed from traditional demographic categories. Things like gender, age, geography, income. Or in the earlier examples, your military service or alumni status.

We did this because traditional demographics were easy to observe AND, equally important, there was an easy way to "find" and reach each of the groups we identified. Age is a perfect example. It isn't difficult to differentiate between a 19-year-old and a septuagenarian. And, of course, it isn't hard to find places where each of these age-based "tribes" likes to hang out.

But the explosive growth of online social networks is dramatically changing all this.

Social networks are an integral part of people's everyday lives. For an increasing number of people, social networks are often the first thing they check in the morning and the last thing they visit at night. Moreover, these social networks not only enable people to find each other; they encourage connections. Each network's viability relies on it!

And in doing so, social networks enable and sustain the ability for new, modern tribal communities to develop and evolve.

But here's the most important thing to know about these new tribal dynamics. Because much of it is played out in open forums and in real time, people are not only able to "find" these new tribes in order to become members, but organizations of every size and shape—from the multinational Fortune 100 firm to the small community nonprofit—have the opportunity to connect and engage with each member of the tribe individually.

That is why tribes are so important today.

MOTIVATIONS FOR BEING PART OF A COMMUNITY OR "TRIBE"

If communities and tribes are expanding, the first question to ask is, "why?" What is motivating people's desire to join modern-day tribes? If we know why people form communities and tribes, we are better positioned to know how to listen, talk, engage, and build relationships with them.

To help discover what was behind the rise of tribes, we asked members to give us the three words that best describe why they are part of groups and communities outside of work and home.

By far, the most important motivator was simple "friendship." But after that, there were significant differences based on life stage.

RELEVANCE

For **Millennials**, the next two most important relevance factors were "having fun" and "learning." Millennials are looking for a good time while growing their career skills.

For **Xers**, the two most common responses were "support" and "learning." This makes sense. They are often at the stage in life when they are both taking care of their kids, along with their aging parents. So, while they too need to advance their careers, they are also in sore need of help with everything from daycare to eldercare.

Boomers share the Millennial's desire for "fun" but are as motivated simply by having "a sense of belonging." We've seen this in other work we've done. One of the many struggles that many retirees face (According to the Insurance Retirement Institute, which represents the annuity industry, just about half of Baby Boomers are now retired—and that is only increasing. Some 10,000 Boomers retire every day.) is the feeling that they are no longer relevant or needed. For them, groups and tribes give them a sense of meaning and purpose.

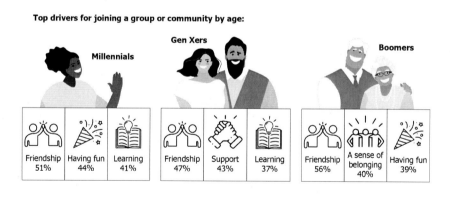

Top drivers for joining a group or community by age:

Millennials
| Friendship 51% | Having fun 44% | Learning 41% |

Gen Xers
| Friendship 47% | Support 43% | Learning 37% |

Boomers
| Friendship 56% | A sense of belonging 40% | Having fun 39% |

A WORLD OF SHARED EXPERIENCE AND INTERESTS

If these are the motivators, what are the dynamics of how groups are forming?

In our study, we identified a sizable block of people who "self-associate" and "self-organize" around shared experiences and interests.

We asked people what percentage of their friends shared most, or all, of their views and preferences in the eight different areas listed below. In five of those eight categories—food, politics, the arts, faith, and exercise—nearly one-third of respondents said that most or all of their friends share their views and preferences. Only about one-in-five said the same thing about sports teams, fashion, and finance.

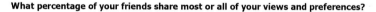

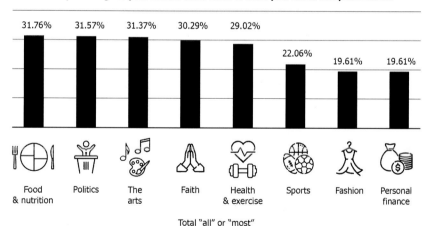

What percentage of your friends share most or all of your views and preferences?

Food & nutrition	Politics	The arts	Faith	Health & exercise	Sports	Fashion	Personal finance
31.76%	31.57%	31.37%	30.29%	29.02%	22.06%	19.61%	19.61%

Total "all" or "most"

This suggests that:

A) There are a lot of people who hang out and associate with people who are spending more and more of their life every day on social media.

B) Social media has made it remarkably easy to find people with like interests.

DIGGING DEEPER

If you look at the responses by life stage, things get more interesting. You might think that the younger you are, the more likely you'll have friends with varied and different interests and that the longer you live, the more likely you'll narrow those friendships to people who share your views.

You would be wrong.

Our data suggests that younger Millennials are much more likely to have friends who share their views than those at later life stages. (The only exception is when it comes to politics.)

Another surprising twist. While you might expect to see Millennials' tribal tendencies in the arts—music, movies, etc.—two of the biggest similarities among friends are food and fitness. Nearly half (49%) of Millennials said their friends most shared their views on food and nutrition. More than two-in-five Millennials (42%) said the same about health and exercise. Indeed, Millennials are more likely to have shared interests in those areas than in matters of religion and faith.

Perhaps not as surprising are gender differences. Men are more likely to hang out with those who share their views on sports, while women are more likely to be friends with people who share their views on food, the arts, faith, and fashion.

HOW RELATIONSHIPS FORM

Beyond self-association, there is the issue of relationships and meaningfulness. How are relationships formed, and how do they relate to a personal sense of fulfillment and happiness? We looked at many different types of relationships, and not surprisingly, the most important by far was family.

But beyond family, we saw evidence that some of the strongest and most meaningful relationships were not being made at the office or in the neighborhood but rather through shared experiences and interests.

Here's how we asked the question:

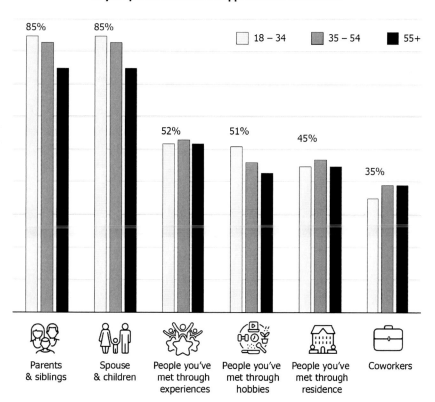

How important are your relationships with these groups and individuals to your personal sense of happiness and fulfillment?

18 – 34   35 – 54   55+

85%   85%   52%   51%   45%   35%

Parents & siblings | Spouse & children | People you've met through experiences | People you've met through hobbies | People you've met through residence | Coworkers

Total "extremely" or "very" important

RELEVANCE

As you can see, these "experienced-based" relationships are particularly important to Millennials. In our study, Millennials consistently exhibited a greater focus and importance on relationships of all types. In fact, they appeared to put as much importance on relationships they form through a night out at a restaurant or doing a sporting activity as they do on the relationships they make through faith-based activities.

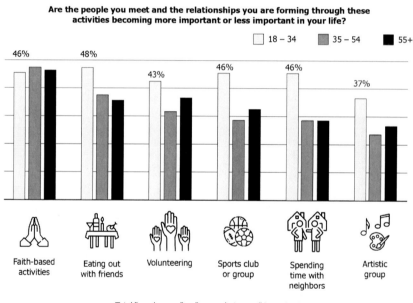

Are the people you meet and the relationships you are forming through these activities becoming more important or less important in your life?

Legend: 18 – 34 | 35 – 54 | 55+

46% | 48% | 43% | 46% | 46% | 37%

Faith-based activities | Eating out with friends | Volunteering | Sports club or group | Spending time with neighbors | Artistic group

Total "much more" or "somewhat more" important

SOCIAL NETWORKS:
THE FUEL BEHIND THE GROWTH OF "TRIBES"

The big difference today is that all these experiences can be shared, consumed, and animated through social networks. In his book, "Tribes: We Need You to Lead Us," Seth Godin noted that today's "always-on" society has a plethora of tools and technologies that facilitate tribal links and that serve as an underpinning of tribal infrastructure on social networks.

We asked people who are active on social networks whether the people they are meeting and the relationships they are forming on those networks are becoming more or less important in their lives.

Of the seven platforms we tested, Facebook was the undisputed king of the tribal landscape. Across all demographics, more than four-in-five said that the relationships they are finding and nurturing on Facebook are becoming of greater importance in their lives.

But after Facebook, the landscape gets much more complicated. The ascendant network for online tribes is Instagram (which happens to be owned by Facebook!). Of the networks we tested, Instagram had the highest growth of meaningful relationships, particularly among Millennial men and women. Nearly half of Millennials (45%) and one-quarter of Xers (25%) say relationships there are becoming more important in their lives.

Relationships made through Instagram, while dominated by Millennial activity, extend well into the Xers. However, relationships through Snapchat appear to be primarily a Millennial phenomenon.

RELEVANCE

Social networks play a critical role in the modern tribal life

Are the people you meet and the relationships you are forming through these channels becoming more or less important in your life? (Total "more important")

Male		Female		18-34		35-54		55+	
Facebook	83%	Facebook	90%	Facebook	89%	Facebook	87%	Facebook	83%
Video game	21%	Instagram	31%	Instagram	45%	Instagram	25%	LinkedIn	21%
LinkedIn	20%	Twitter	19%	Snapchat	31%	Twitter	22%	Video game	19%
Twitter	20%	Snapchat	19%	Twitter	21%	Video game	20%	Twitter	16%
Instagram	16%	Video game	15%	Video game	16%	LinkedIn	16%	Fantasy	9%
Fantasy	13%	LinkedIn	13%	LinkedIn	10%	Snapchat	10%	Instagram	8%
Snapchat	9%	Fantasy	2%	Fantasy	8%	Fantasy	10%	Snapchat	5%

Instagram also has a strong foundation among the emerging "minority-majority" population groups.

The ethnic landscape

Are the people you meet and the relationships you are forming through these channels becoming more or less important in your life? (Total "more important")

White		African American		Hispanic		Asian	
Facebook	87%	Facebook	77%	Facebook	89%	Facebook	85%
Instagram	20%	Instagram	31%	Instagram	44%	Instagram	28%
Twitter	19%	Video game	25%	Snapchat	25%	LinkedIn	28%
Video game	18%	Twitter	22%	Twitter	22%	Twitter	20%
LinkedIn	16%	Snapchat	19%	Video game	16%	Video game	18%
Snapchat	12%	LinkedIn	17%	LinkedIn	11%	Snapchat	8%
Fantasy	9%	Fantasy	8%	Fantasy	8%	Fantasy	3%

A QUICK LOOK AT GEN Z

Anyone born between 1981 and 1996 is considered a Millennial, and anyone born from 1997 onward is part of a new generation, Generation Z (Gen Z).

Since Gen Zers have grown up having social networks as a central part of their lives, we decided to take a deep dive to learn what these folks are all about to better understand tribes.

We began with an important question that marketers have. What will it take for brands to resonate with them? As you will see, corporate responsibility, broadly defined, is extremely important.

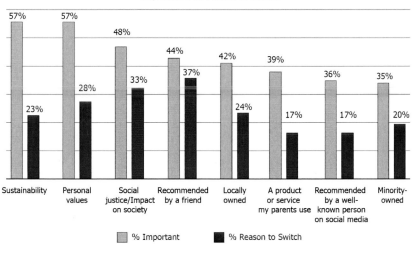

What it Takes for Brands to Break Through to Gen Z

When you are considering purchasing a product or service, how important is it to know that the company behind the product is:

In the past year, have you switched from one product or service to another because you learned the new product or service was any of the following? Please select all that apply.

Question Type: Single Matrix | Total Respondents: 511
Question Type: Multi Select | Total Respondents: 511

Importance vs. Reason to Switch

Category	% Important	% Reason to Switch
Sustainability	57%	23%
Personal values	57%	28%
Social justice/Impact on society	48%	33%
Recommended by a friend	44%	37%
Locally owned	42%	24%
A product or service my parents use	39%	17%
Recommended by a well-known person on social media	36%	17%
Minority-owned	35%	20%

RELEVANCE

For brands to connect with Gen Z, going green, having strong values, and focusing on social justice are important for purchase consideration and brand conversion.

Well over half say a company's commitment to sustainability is important to them when considering purchasing a product or service.

A similar majority say the same thing about the company's alignment to their personal values, and nearly half noted commitment to social justice is important.

When it comes to brand conversion, word of mouth remains king. In the past year, more than one-third of Gen Zers say they have switched brands based on a friend's recommendation. That is followed by societal impact—a third has switched to a different brand in the past year because they learned the company was making a positive impact on society.

If a company's actions and reputation were so important, we wondered where members of Gen Z would learn about these things.

The answer, perhaps, not surprisingly, was social media.

Social Media as a Source for News

Thinking about how you get news about current events, which of the following best describes how
much of that news comes from social media?

Which of the following social media platforms do you turn to the most for news about current events?

Which of the following social media platforms do you trust the most as a source of news about
current events?

**How Much News Comes from
Social Media**

**Social Media Used for News vs.
Most Trusted for News**

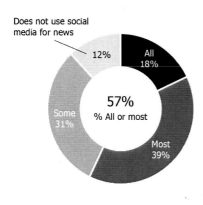

Does not use social
media for news

12%

All
18%

57%
% All or most

Some
31%

Most
39%

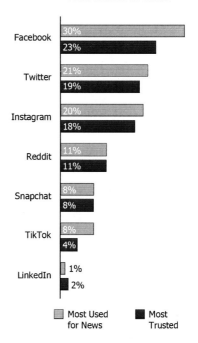

Facebook 30% / 23%

Twitter 21% / 19%

Instagram 20% / 18%

Reddit 11% / 11%

Snapchat 8% / 8%

TikTok 8% / 4%

LinkedIn 1% / 2%

Most Used for News — Most Trusted

Question Type: Single Choice
Total Respondents: 511

Question Type: Single Choice
Reduced Base, Shares News on Social Media: 449

RELEVANCE

In the era of "fake news," a majority of Gen Z gets all or most of their news from social media—most notably from Facebook.

• Well over half of Gen Zers gets all or most of their news from social media.

• Among those that get news from social media, about a third turn to Facebook and one-fifth turn to Twitter or Instagram.

• When it comes to social media they trust, about one-fourth say they trust Facebook the most for news.

What naturally follows from that is when someone shares an article with them that they strongly agree with, Gen Zers will share it.

Sharing News on Social Media

When someone you follow on social media shares a news article you strongly agree with, how often do you share it?

Of the following, which is the top reason you share articles or news stories on social media?

Sharing News on Social Media

Never 15%
Every time 14%
Some of the time 21%
64% % At least half of the time
Most of the time 28%
Half of the time 23%

Question Type: Single Choice
Total Respondents: 511

Reason to Share News on Social Media

To raise awareness — 38%
To voice my opinion — 22%
To let others know my interests — 20%
I don't share news on social media — 20%

Sharing news on social media is commonplace for Gen Zers, and they mostly do so to raise awareness.

- About two-thirds share news they strongly agree with at least half the time.

- Just over a third say they share news on social media to raise awareness of a topic or issue.

- Another one-fifth share news because they want to voice their opinion or let others know their interests.

But here is something to keep an eye on: This reliance on social media may not be forever.

RELEVANCE

Future Social Media Usage

In the next year, which of the following are you most likely to do?

Which of the following, if any, are reasons you would consider permanently deleting your personal social media accounts? Please select all that apply.

Social Media Usage within the Next Year

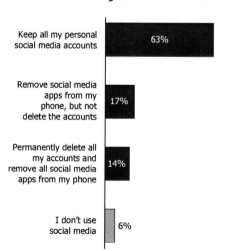

Social Media Usage within the Next Year	
Keep all my personal social media accounts	63%
Remove social media apps from my phone, but not delete the accounts	17%
Permanently delete all my accounts and remove all social media apps from my phone	14%
I don't use social media	6%

Reason to Delete Social Media	
Mental health and wellbeing	52%
Reduce time spent on social media	44%
Data privacy and protection concerns	38%
Reduce the need to always be connected	29%
Distrust in news and information on social media	26%
None of the above	11%

Question Type: Single Choice | Total Respondents: 511
Question Type: Multi Select | Reduced Base, Uses Social Media: 480

Social media has a stronghold on Gen Z. Most do not see themselves changing their social media habits in the near future.

However, if they were to delete social media, alleviating digital fatigue and data privacy concerns could be a reason.

[Continued]

- About two-thirds of Gen Z are likely to keep all their social media accounts within the next year.
- However, if they considered deleting their social media accounts, about half would do so for mental health and well-being or to reduce time spent on social media.
- There is some level of distrust in social media – a third say they would delete social media for data privacy, and another one-fourth would delete because of their distrust of the news on social media.

INFLUENCERS CAN FOSTER RELEVANCE AND STRENGTHEN TRIBES

Increasingly, influencers drive the social and earned media (which used to be called free media or media exposure, is publicity gained through promotional efforts other than paid media advertising) landscape, using their blogs and large social media followings to advise consumers on which products to buy and how to live a lifestyle similar to their own.

Like traditional media, online influencers often specialize in particular audience segments. For example, a set of influencers may give advice specifically to mothers, and another set may specialize in offering vacation advice to travelers.

To over-simplify, we can put influencers into three categories, as the following graphic shows:

RELEVANCE

The Three Types of Influencers

Mega-Influencers | 1M+ Followers
Celebrities who can generate tremendous reach and engagement

Macro-Influencers | 100K – 1M Followers
Highly regarded bloggers and online personalities. Because they tend to focus on specific topics, they offer high relevance in distinct categories

Micro-Influencers | 10K – 50K Followers
Comprising the majority of social media users, micro-influencers reach fewer people, but their authenticity and trustworthiness makes them quite capable of swaying the opinions of others

Source: Mavrck

You can see the benefits of each with the next graphic.

Benefits Of Each Influencer Type

Mega
Quantity: 0.001% of content creators & prodigies, ~5K across social networks
Reach: 1M+ with 2%-5% engaged per post
Relevance: Higher topical relevance; lower brand relevance
Resonance: Lowest ability to drive a desired action from audience

Macro
Quantity: 1% who create authentic, engaging content, ~32K across social networks
Reach: 100K-1M with 5%-25% engaged per post
Relevance: Higher topical relevance; lower brand relevance
Resonance: Moderate ability to drive a desired action from audience

Micro
Quantity: 9% who amplify content, ~15M across social networks
Reach: 10K-50K with 25%-50% engaged per post
Relevance: Lower topical relevance; higher brand relevance
Resonance: Highest ability to drive a desired action from audience

Source: Mavrck

INFLUENCERS APPROACH: A FIVE-STEP PLAN

How do you incorporate influencers into your marketing program? We suggest the following five-step approach.

- **Set parameters.** Determine specific goals, objectives, and priorities for your influencer program.

- **Determine how you are going to find them.** Scour earned and social coverage, looking for conversation drivers. Leverage tools such as Traackr, Meltwater, Radian 6, and Compete.

- **Define influence.** You are looking for an influencer to have three things: *Reach* (they have a large audience); *Authority* (they are experts in their fields—when they speak, others listen); and *Relevance* (they are relevant to your brand or message).

- **Group "like influencers" together** based on how you want to engage with them.

- **Determine approach.** Figure out outreach strategies and what you are going to ask them to do.

PUTTING THEM TO WORK FOR YOU

Having identified the people you are trying to reach, you want them to help spread the word about what you have. Obviously, you will determine what works best for you. But the following can give you an idea of what the process could be like.

RELEVANCE

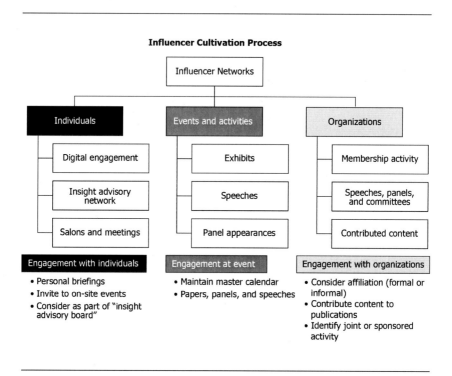

Influencer Cultivation Process

Influencer Networks

Individuals	Events and activities	Organizations
Digital engagement	Exhibits	Membership activity
Insight advisory network	Speeches	Speeches, panels, and committees
Salons and meetings	Panel appearances	Contributed content

Engagement with individuals
- Personal briefings
- Invite to on-site events
- Consider as part of "insight advisory board"

Engagement at event
- Maintain master calendar
- Papers, panels, and speeches

Engagement with organizations
- Consider affiliation (formal or informal)
- Contribute content to publications
- Identify joint or sponsored activity

As consumers become more disenchanted with advertisements and celebrity endorsements, brands look toward new social media influencers for authenticity and targeted messages.

SHARED EXPERIENCES, SHARED INTERESTS, AND BRANDS

So, what does all this mean for marketers?

To find out, we looked at seventy brands across seven different sectors—retail, hospitality, automotive, food and beverage, apparel, consumer electronics, and nonprofits.

We then identified "brand champions," people who said that brand was their "favorite" among all the others listed in the sector.

We then looked at the profile of these brand champions based on:

A) The likelihood that their friends shared their views and preferences.

B) The importance they put on relationships made through shared experiences.

What we found was that brands tended to attract certain clusters and have a particular tribal profile.

Take retail. Walmart fans were 23 percent more likely to put high importance on relationships they made through faith-based activities. That is, Walmart attracts more people of faith. But Walmart fans were also 18 percent more likely to have friends who share their views and preferences on fashion. Now you might not think Walmart is the most fashionable of brands, but what this suggests is that, among Walmart fans, there is a particular look that they tend to share. So, Walmart might want to understand what "fashion" means to its supporters and how that might translate into a communications or marketing strategy.

RELEVANCE

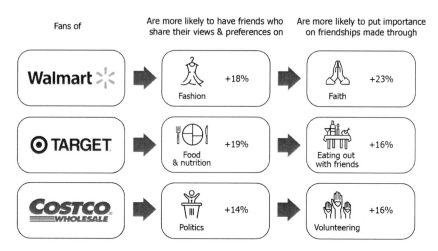

Fans of	Are more likely to have friends who share their views & preferences on	Are more likely to put importance on friendships made through
Walmart	Fashion +18%	Faith +23%
TARGET	Food & nutrition +19%	Eating out with friends +16%
COSTCO WHOLESALE	Politics +14%	Volunteering +16%

Among clusters or tribes, % consumers who selected this brand as their most preferred retail brand among ten other retailers compared to a national average.

Compare that to the community or tribal profiles of some food and beverage companies, notably Coca-Cola. Fans of Coke also over-index on having friends who share their tastes in fashion. But they also put above-average importance on friendships formed through the arts. The latter (arts) may say a lot about the former (fashion), which means that the Coke "fashion" tribe may look a lot different than that of Walmart's.

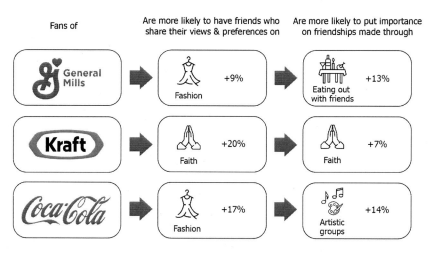

Fans of

Are more likely to have friends who share their views & preferences on

Are more likely to put importance on friendships made through

General Mills	Fashion	+9%	Eating out with friends	+13%
Kraft	Faith	+20%	Faith	+7%
Coca-Cola	Fashion	+17%	Artistic groups	+14%

Among clusters or tribes, % consumers who selected this brand as their most preferred retail brand among ten other retailers compared to a national average.

Then there are the profiles of the fans of two leading consumer electronics companies—Apple and Samsung. One appears defined by athletics and healthy eating (Apple) and the other by fashion and entertainment (Samsung).

That alone would suggest some very different strategies when looking to activate and energize the base of each brand.

RELEVANCE

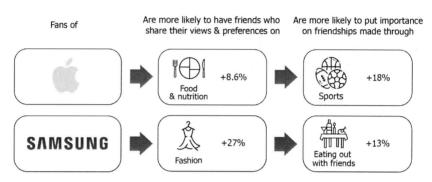

Among clusters or tribes, % consumers who selected this brand as their most preferred retail brand among ten other retailers compared to a national average.

As we went through this analysis, we discovered four brands that could be labeled "trans-tribal:" Amazon, General Motors, Levi Strauss, and The Salvation Army. These are brands whose fans are least likely to have friends that share their views and preferences in each of the eight areas we tested.

What could account for this "trans-tribal" quality?

Scale might be one. They are all global brands that may not dominate their category but certainly are vital to defining it.

Generational relevance might be another reason. Each brand is as familiar and iconic among Millennials as they are among Xers and Boomers.

Similarly, lifestyle transcendence might be another. These are brands that appeal to every station, walk of life, and ideology.

Then there is time and history. These trans-tribal brands weren't created yesterday. Of the four, Amazon is the "baby," having been founded more than 25 years ago (1994). But the other three have been at their craft for well over a century—General Motors (1908), Levi Strauss (1853), and Salvation Army (1865).

Why this matters: Understanding tribes is essential for
individuals, brands, causes, and candidates who would engage
a consumer, customer, or prospective follower in hopes of
persuading them to buy, donate, vote, or take action today.

The takeaway from all this: Any brand, candidate, or advocate
for a cause must understand tribes and find a way to participate in
tribal formation and activity. It's how many people, Millennials
foremost, navigate their world.

In part, the growing number of tribes could be in response to
the sense of individual isolation that Harvard professor Robert D.
Putnam identified in 2000 with his book "Bowling Alone: The
Collapse and Revival of American Community." (And, indeed,
professor Putnam argues today that the trend has now gone the
other way, and there is a growing sense of connectedness.)

But another reason could be it is a reaction to the stress people
feel. Our collective anxiety is growing.

Consider:

- **Money.** An increasing number of people are **losing sleep
  these days over their financial situation.**
- **Work.** People are **less confident that they could find a new
  job** within six months if they were to lose their current job.
- **Raw deal!** Seven in 10 Americans think the **U.S. economic
  system is "rigged"** in favor of certain groups.

A LOOK INSIDE THE NUMBERS

In light of this, it could be that more and more of us are coming together in groups and tribes as a coping mechanism. Moving forward, we believe that continued anxiety and uncertainty in society and the workplace will make tribes or communities much more important in people's day-to-day lives.

We see evidence of this when we look at correlations between overall optimism and the importance of shared experiences. You'll remember that Millennials are at the vanguard of tribal formation. Well, guess what? In our study, they were—by far—the most optimistic.

While we live in a time where pessimism abounds, most of that pessimism comes from the older generations. When asked how confident they were that things will improve in the United States, from one-quarter to one-third of Millennials said they were "very confident" about future progress. That was far ahead of the confidence levels of either Xers or Boomers.

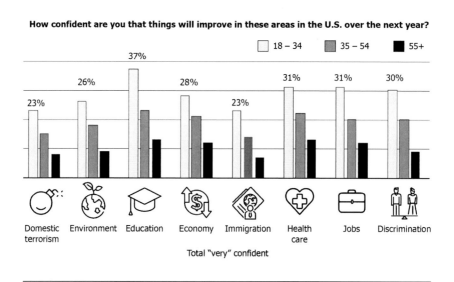

How confident are you that things will improve in these areas in the U.S. over the next year?

18 – 34   35 – 54   55+

Domestic terrorism   Environment   Education   Economy   Immigration   Health care   Jobs   Discrimination

Total "very" confident

As we've seen, tribe formation results from the eternal yearning to connect and youthful optimism that the connection will be valuable. Experiences or interests provide the glue.

THIS SHOULDN'T BE SURPRISING

The concept of tribes fits in perfectly with our relevance model. Remember, we have said, relevance is the full experience of a person, group, brand, product, idea, or interest sufficient to not only change minds but behaviors. To be relevant, an entity must satisfy the yearning for connection by activating at least one—and at best all four—relevance pathways: thinking, sensory, values, and community impulses. Tribal activity does exactly that. It is another way of getting through to the people we would like to be our customers.

Relevance Pathway	Tribal Traits
Thinking	Shared Interests
Sensory	Experiences
Values	Passion
Community	Friendship

The consideration of tribes needs to be an integral part of your marketing efforts.

What specifically should you do? Let us give you five ideas:

RELEVANCE

- Closely examine the shared experiences and interests of brand champions.

- Continually re-examine how these shared-experience relationships are being formed and fostered through social media channels, and tailor your social network engagement accordingly.

- Identify other ways to configure marketing and communications strategies to strengthen and deepen shared-experience and interest connections.

- Look for opportunities in "tribal adjacencies," other shared-experience and shared-interest groups that align both with the brand and with current brand champions.

- Reconfigure segmentation and targeting strategy around shared experience and interest.

TAKEAWAYS FROM CHAPTER 5

1. **Identify your target audience's passions** *and* provide ways for your target audience to come together around one of those passions. That will form a tribe.

2. **Provide experiences the tribe can share together.** Give the tribe many ways to be together (e.g., real-world events and online communities).

3. **Make it easy for the tribe to embrace new members.** You always want to try to grow the tribe if you can; if it makes sense.

4. **Make the tribe visible.** A proud tribe wants to be seen.

6

Combining Everything We Just Discussed in Section I

Let's take a step back.

We've covered a lot of ground in the first five chapters. We began by talking about the people you are trying to reach, and we came to see that they have even more filters in place than you imagined to block unwanted messages, making your job of reaching them much more difficult.

The way to get through those filters, we have learned, is to know what your customers are looking for and understand how they want to be approached.

They always want to be engaged through one (or more) of the following ways:

Thinking

After hearing your message, they say things like "this product/ service/idea…"

- "Helps me meet my needs."

- "Helps make my life easier."

Community

In response to your idea, they say things like:

- "Being associated with this product/service/idea makes me feel better about myself."

- "I want people to know I am associated with it."

RELEVANCE

Values

After thinking about what you have to say, they respond:

- "I associate the message/product/service/idea with values important to me."

- "It stands for the same things I do."

Sensory

Your communications get them to say:

- "I like the feeling when I'm around this product/service or idea."

- "It inspires me."

We saw that those eight filters naturally fall into the four quadrants above: thinking, community, values, and sensory.

In our first book, we said when taken together, those four quadrants make up a model that we call "the Relevance Egg."

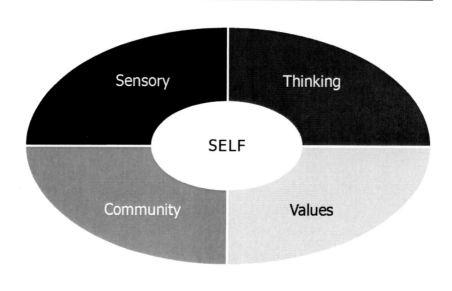

As you can see, the people we are trying to reach are at the center of the egg. The more ways you can engage with them, the better your chances of being heard.

Once we are aware of the drivers of behavior that make up the Relevance Egg, we can go deeper to forge connections by looking for relevance clusters, a group of varied people united solely by common purpose or experience.

All this makes sense, of course. But what marketers and communicators want to know is how to put these ideas into practice to better serve customers. Explaining how to do just that is what we are going to do in the chapters ahead that make up the second part of the book.

Specifically, we are going to look at companies and nonprofits that have used relevance to differentiate themselves in the marketplace. And then, because not everything is within an organization's control, we are going to take a look at a handful of big issues to see where relevance could help solve the problem.

By the time we are done, you will have a series of strategies that have been proven to work when it comes to changing minds and behavior, strategies that will help you stay ahead of the competition.

SECTION II.
CASE STUDIES

7

FM Global

How Do You Make an Insurance Company Relevant?

Invariably, when we begin talking about connecting with customers by being relevant, we always hear this from one skeptic in the crowd: "You mean to tell me that you can make any company relevant? Prove it. Tell me how it would work with something like a commercial property insurance company? How would you make them relevant?"

We're glad you asked.

Read on.

Okay, here's your challenge: figure out a way to make a monoline insurance company top-of-mind and meaningful.

Sure, this happens all the time when something bad occurs. When you or your company have to file a claim because of a fire, natural disaster, or the like, for example. When those things (unfortunately) happen, the company that insures you is immediately relevant. In fact, until things get back to normal, the insurance company you do business with is one of the most important relationships in your life.

But how does a commercial insurance company make itself relevant when things are going well for its clients—and the companies it would like to be its clients—and those executives are concentrating on more pressing things than making sure they are covered fully? Yes, of course, those busy people agree that

RELEVANCE

insurance is important, but there are products to ship, services to provide, quarterly numbers to make, and deadlines seemingly every hour. Insurance is way down on the bottom of the list of what they are paying attention to.

Since that is the case, how do you make yourself relevant to them if you are an insurance company?

That was the challenge that FM Global faced. This case study was created in 2019, and the company's marketing strategies continue to evolve.

FM Global, which began life in 1835 as Factory Mutuals, is a Rhode Island-based mutual commercial property insurance company with offices worldwide specializing in insurance and loss prevention services (more on that in a minute) provided primarily to large corporations around the globe. In 2020, it was ranked #1 and "the most highly regarded insurer in property claims handling," according to a survey of hundreds of risk managers by Advisen Ltd., a leading insurance information and analytics firm.

All that is good, but it does not make you relevant.

To become so, FM Global began by looking at its branding and positioning statement, which captured what it was trying to communicate to clients and potential clients. The company's tagline: "When you're resilient, you're in business."

That statement is compelling because the word "resilience" has an emotional resonance both personally and commercially. But it was clearly the business part of the tagline the company was interested in.

A resilient business is one that performs under pressure. And it is one that bounces back should a disaster hit. So, resilience as the starting point for a leading insurance company—one that was high-performing itself—seemed right.

The key to relevant differentiation for FM Global would be

showing how resilience leads to improved business performance, sharing how companies need to get and stay in top shape in order to adapt to a rapidly evolving, unpredictable, and volatile world.

This argument played to the company's strength. With a 180-year-plus history, FM Global is a credible leader in the dialogue about resilience. (You don't last that long if you are not.) More importantly, the way the company does business supported that message.

"As an insurance company, we are very, very different," says FM Global's Assistant Vice President of Public Relations, Steven Zenofsky. "We're not just an insurance company who pays out on a loss. Of course, we'll do that, but we are focused on helping our clients—our policyholders, who are our owners—to hopefully not have the property loss to begin with."

The company does this by having its engineers analyze a company's business by looking for potential vulnerabilities. Says Zenofsky: "Our fundamental belief is that the majority of property loss is preventable, not inevitable."

Now, does this positioning make FM Global instantly relevant to all major companies who need commercial property insurance? Obviously not.

There are always going to be some customers who say, "the reason I have insurance is to pay for a loss. I don't want bells and whistles. I don't want engineering and analysis. I want the most coverage for the lowest price. Period." Clearly, FM Global's positioning will never be relevant to them. But that's fine. You can't be relevant to everyone unless you are offering a commodity like electricity. If you try, you'll end up with a weak message that will resonate with no one.

"We're on the opposite end of the spectrum from people who just want low-cost, no-frills insurance," says Zenofsky. "You've got a segment that says, 'If I get a check from an insurance company, bad things have already occurred, and I can't afford for that to happen to my business because: I could lose competitiveness; I could lose market share; I could lose a product line; my reputation could be damaged; it could have an effect on shareholder value; etc.' The list of horrible things that could happen just goes on and on. And so, they're very, very focused on prevention. We're very relevant to that segment, and we have long-term relationships spanning a hundred years or more with clients who have that philosophy, which happens to be the philosophy of our business. It's in our DNA, it's who we are, and it's baked into our business model, and it meshes perfectly with what these clients want.

"And then there is a third segment of the market," says Zenofsky. "It's where you're trying to help people understand the value of FM Global's business model to them, especially if they have not considered it, or if they've got preconceptions, or they have misconceptions about what we do, or they see all insurers as the same."

In that situation, the company clearly could be relevant if it could explain its unique approach designed to prevent loss and its commitment to get the insured back to normal—to help them be resilient—should a loss occur.

Here's an example of that. St. John's Regional Medical Center in Joplin, Missouri, took a direct hit from a tornado that rotated one of the hospital's towers four inches off its foundation. (The hospital, soon thereafter, was considered structurally unsound and razed.)

"We were on site immediately," Zenofsky recalls. "I think we gave them an advance check of $50 million just so they could start rebuilding and be able to provide care for the community, while we were processing the claim, and then our engineers worked with them to rebuild a more robust hospital."

WE'RE UNDERWAY

So far, so good. It was clear that FM Global could be relevant to a large number of people.

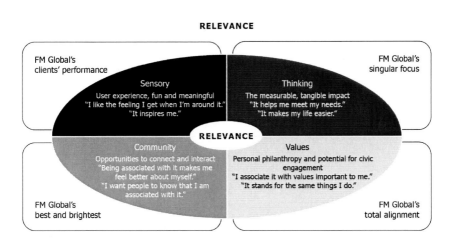

But where would it fit within the relevance egg? As you can see on the surface, it could seemingly fit anywhere within the four quadrants.

That could be fine, of course. You can try to go after people who fall into all four quadrants if that makes sense. But while you never want to turn away potential customers, you do want your message to fit as closely as possible to what they need and want. **If you try to be relevant to everyone, you will end up appealing to no one.**

Company executives thought it through and decided it was clear that the positioning worked best in the sensory and values quadrants.

RELEVANCE

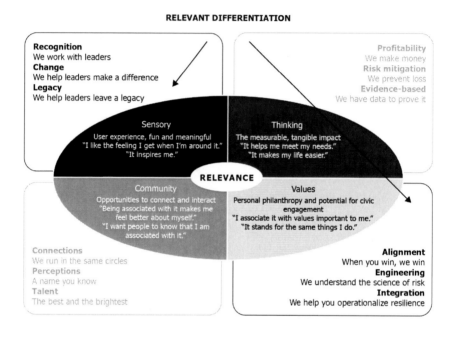

RELEVANT DIFFERENTIATION

Recognition
We work with leaders
Change
We help leaders make a difference
Legacy
We help leaders leave a legacy

Profitability
We make money
Risk mitigation
We prevent loss
Evidence-based
We have data to prove it

Sensory
User experience, fun and meaningful
"I like the feeling I get when I'm around it."
"It inspires me."

Thinking
The measurable, tangible impact
"It helps me meet my needs."
"It makes my life easier."

RELEVANCE

Community
Opportunities to connect and interact
"Being associated with it makes me
feel better about myself."
"I want people to know that I am
associated with it."

Values
Personal philanthropy and potential for civic
engagement
"I associate it with values important to me."
"It stands for the same things I do."

Connections
We run in the same circles
Perceptions
A name you know
Talent
The best and the brightest

Alignment
When you win, we win
Engineering
We understand the science of risk
Integration
We help you operationalize resilience

Sensory because the argument "I like the feeling that I get when I am around it" was clearly how clients felt about the company. They liked the fact that FM Global was focused on loss prevention and a quick recovery.

And that message truly was underscored by the "values" quadrant. Clients *really* liked FM Global because "it stands for the same things I do," and the phrase "I associate it with values that are important to me" both fit perfectly.

In fact, the conclusion that FM Global's strongest positioning could fall in the values quadrant fit perfectly with how the company was thinking of itself.

Here are the seven ways FM Global believes it is different and where those differences fit within the relevance egg.

116

The language is theirs. We are just pointing out, in the parentheses, where the company's positioning fits within the relevance egg:

- **Rapid Claims Response (Thinking, Values).** Our clients know that time is money, and a quick settlement of claims satisfies this very rational calculus. Rapid claims response also affirms the shared values of client service, satisfaction, and commitment to the relationship. FM Global delivers on all of these fronts.

- **Supportive Client Partnerships (Values, Sensory).** Clients tangibly sense FM Global's commitment to this core value, i.e., keeping them in business versus simply transferring risk. Clients literally see, hear, and feel the commitment during site visits by our loss prevention consultants and when they visit our Research Campus to help them understand their risks.

- **Loss Prevention Engineering (Thinking, Values).** Most clients appreciate data-driven recommendations, based on scientific research, that will keep them in business, and no one delivers this better than FM Global.

- **Global Delivery (Thinking, Community).** It's a black-and-white business need: Our clients need their commercial insurance provider to deliver seamless, consistent, and compliant coverage wherever they operate. FM Global delivers this across 62,000 locations in 130+ countries.

- **Mutual Ownership (Community, Values, Thinking).** This differentiator activates at least three of the four relevance pathways. Our policyholders are our owners, so they can be assured we are solely focused on their best interests. Our mutual structure makes a de facto community of clients/owners invested in the company's success. It ensures that the values of clients and the insurance company are fully aligned, which isn't always the case in a traditional shareholder structure. This alignment makes good business sense.

- **Business Risk Consulting (Thinking, Values).** CFOs, generally speaking, really don't care about much beyond their share price and revenue stream. Our Business Risk Consulting group can help connect FM Global with these two key values of the economic buyer by logically demonstrating how a deeper understanding of their business vulnerabilities and exposures can protect key revenue streams, minimize business interruption, and preserve reputation. Providing this insight via our Business Impact Analysis (BIA) gives CFOs the rational, fact-based information they require in addressing the thinking relevance quadrant.

- **Specialty Company (Values, Community).** FM Global is a monoline insurer and offers one thing and one thing only–engineering-driven property insurance. This differentiator is important as it gives FM Global the ability to focus, not only on its own business but on the business of its clients. Not being distracted by multiple product lines, or having the need to develop new products to please shareholders, as our competitors do, means FM Global has the time and dedication to remain a leader in global property insurance. As a monoline insurer specializing in commercial property insurance and backed by an engineering force that creates a strong business model, our aim is to know our clients' businesses, their property exposures, and where we can add business value.

Zenofsky gives an example of how this plays out in practice. "Take loss prevention engineering. That's one of the major things that makes us different. We've aligned the differentiator of loss prevention engineering to the values quadrant. We try to demonstrate our relevance to those clients who appreciate data-driven sound recommendations that keep them in business because nobody can do that better than FM Global. So that speaks to how they think and what they value.

"We've tried to take each of our differentiators and structure them around relevance," he adds.

PUTTING IT INTO PRACTICE

And so, the groundwork was created for making FM Global relevant. When asked what makes the company different from other insurance companies, executives could say:

We do one thing, and we do it better than anyone in the world. We make our customers and their people more resilient, which keeps them performing at a high level.

As a monoline business, FM Global is singularly focused on keeping our customers' lights on and doors open, both in good times and in bad.

We have knowledge from being a valued partner for thousands of companies for the last 180 years. When a catastrophe puts your business performance on the line, you need a partner who has the knowledge and expertise to make a difference when it really counts.

This kind of focus helps FM Global attract new clients.

"When we start talking about loss prevention engineering and investments and what can threaten your business from a property perspective, we're talking about a low-frequency, high-severity event that may not happen during the career of the financial executive who is responsible for choosing us. But chances are, at some point, if that organization is unprepared, it's going to happen," Zenofsky says.

"So, there is a gap. And what we're constantly trying to do is dial up the relevance of property risk and pay attention to property risk for multinational organizations and say this really needs to be on that financial executive's agenda because here's the consequences if it is not.

"Tying it back to our unique engineering approach, we're trying to develop engineering offerings that speak more to the senior financial executive, and in their language as well, so we're not just talking about putting a flood barrier in place or putting in more sprinklers, but being able to show them in dollars and cents what this could mean for their organization if they aren't well protected.

"So, it's really trying to connect those dots from the wonky engineering to the dollars and cents that senior financial executives care about," according to Zenofsky.

In other words, making FM Global relevant.

THIS FITS IN PERFECTLY

As we have seen, focusing on relevance gave FM Global a framework for what it was already doing.

"I always feel that the target audience, whoever our target audience may be, is governed by three filters," Zenofsky says:

- So what?
- What's in it for me?
- Why should I care?

"No matter whether it's the media or our audience, those are the three questions I'm always trying to answer when we're filtering things and trying to tailor our communication to make that relevant to our audience. You answer those questions, and you make sure that you understand your target audience, and understand that these are the three things that they're evaluating," he adds. "If you can't do an effective job at answering those questions from their perspective, then you're out.

"So, the fact that we now have this framework here around relevance helped us find other ways to be thinking about opportunities where we could have touchpoints, through these quadrants, through these lenses, that we had not necessarily considered before."

RELEVANCE

TAKEAWAYS FROM CHAPTER 7

1. **Any company, an insurance company included,** can find a way to be relevant by getting through the filters potential customers have in place. If FM Global can do it, you can do it too.

2. **You can't force the fit.** If you say you are relevant to a customer, you really must be relevant. There is no faster way to lose credibility than to promise something you can't—or don't—deliver.

3. **Conversely, don't try to appeal to everyone.** Trying to reach the widest possible audience requires you to be extremely bland. And bland things are, by definition, commodities. There is no emotional connection to a commodity. Don't believe us? How connected are you to tap water or white sneaker laces? They are commodities and don't offend anyone. But you are not fiercely loyal to them either.

4. **The easiest way to establish a connection with customers** is in the areas where your company is strongest. FM Global built off of their strengths: helping clients eliminate potential losses.

5. **Communicate. Communicate. Communicate.** Stress your relevance to your audience in every single communication with them.

8

Relevance and the Infrastructure Mess

Huge societal problems can seem daunting...because they are.

One way you can start to cut them down to size is by giving people a reason to pay attention to them in a serious way.

America's infrastructure serves as a case in point.

We keep saying we're going to do something about our nation's aging infrastructure.

But we don't.

Rarely has a need with such bipartisan support gone underfunded for so long, despite the diligent efforts of many organizations—from labor to business and even political and policy organizations on the right and left—to break the logjam.

To support an effort on what is one of the biggest economic challenges facing this country, we underwrote a study of the American electorate. Our goal was to find out what voters find relevant in the infrastructure discussion, along with ideas on how to move our infrastructure forward.

The following are five insights gleaned from talking to American voters. It is our hope that this can help fuel interest, enthusiasm, and support for the much-needed investment in our nation's infrastructure.

RELEVANCE

EDUCATING THE PUBLIC

Insight Number 1: Americans don't appreciate the infrastructure problem. At the very least, we need to get through the thinking filter.

Let's go back a few years. In 2016, people who voted for Donald Trump were much more sanguine about our nation's infrastructure than Clinton voters. On every infrastructure element tested, Trump voters were more likely to rate these systems as either being "excellent" (A) or "good" (B) than those who voted for Clinton.

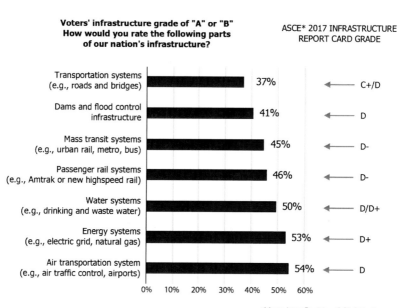

Voters' infrastructure grade of "A" or "B"
How would you rate the following parts of our nation's infrastructure?

ASCE* 2017 INFRASTRUCTURE REPORT CARD GRADE

Category	Voter grade A/B	ASCE Grade
Transportation systems (e.g., roads and bridges)	37%	C+/D
Dams and flood control infrastructure	41%	D
Mass transit systems (e.g., urban rail, metro, bus)	45%	D-
Passenger rail systems (e.g., Amtrak or new highspeed rail)	46%	D-
Water systems (e.g., drinking and waste water)	50%	D/D+
Energy systems (e.g., electric grid, natural gas)	53%	D+
Air transportation system (e.g., air traffic control, airports)	54%	D

*American Society of Civil Engineers

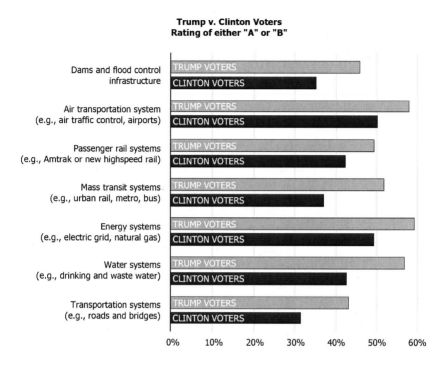

Trump v. Clinton Voters
Rating of either "A" or "B"

There were also age and income disparities. The older you were, the more likely you were to rate our infrastructure positively. The poorer you were, the more likely you were to rate our infrastructure poorly.

> Those most likely to give our infrastructure a poor grade were women, those with lower incomes, and those with less than a college degree.

RELEVANCE

ALIGN INFRASTRUCTURE WITH VOTER PRIORITIES

Insight Number 2: Attention needs to be focused on areas that voters already find important.

Infrastructure covers a lot of territory. By definition, it encompasses all the necessary systems and structures that make business and civic life possible. One of the early challenges for the government will be: where we should focus the investment given limited economic resources.

In our survey, voters provided a clear set of priorities: water, energy, and transportation.

When asked to rank priorities, over half of voters (55%) said that the first or second most important priority was our drinking and wastewater systems. The next most important priority was our energy systems, including our electric grid and natural gas networks. A distant third was transportation, including our roads and bridges.

The public's priorities are largely bipartisan with two modest differences.

Trump voters put considerably more focus than Clinton voters on upgrading our energy systems. Nearly half (45%) of Trump voters felt energy was either the top or second most important priority. By contrast, only a little over a quarter (26%) of Clinton voters felt the same way.

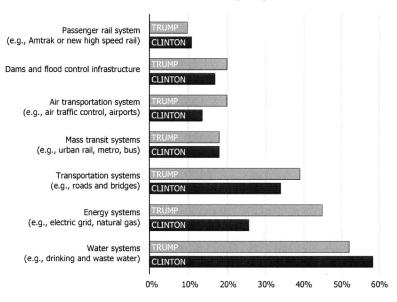

Trump v. Clinton
1st or 2nd infrastructure priority

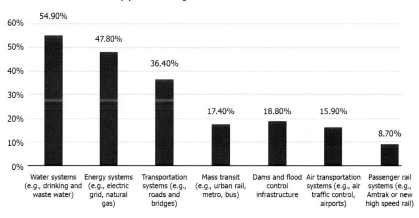

Voters ranking either 1st or 2nd in importance
Rank the top priorities for government investment in infrastructure

RELEVANCE

There were other differences, as well. Trump voters felt stronger about transportation than Clinton voters, while Clinton voters emphasized water systems more than Trump voters.

There are two important things to note.

The data doesn't suggest things like passenger rail, flood control, air transportation, and mass transit systems are unimportant. Rather, it reveals that they were not top priorities of the people surveyed.

Also, as noted earlier, voters give our infrastructure much more positive grades than many experts do. Voters may have this wrong! But if they do, they are going to need more education and engagement to change their views.

> There appears to be (mostly) bipartisan agreement on the major priorities.

RETHINK THE CONVERSATION

Insight Number 3: Make the message as dramatic as the problem.

Let's begin this section with a question: Are we correctly talking about the urgency of this critical issue?

The case for infrastructure typically focuses on productivity and jobs. Improved infrastructure means greater efficiencies, greater access to improved technologies and improved materials, and an overall more efficient and productive economy. By investing in infrastructure, we also create jobs—particularly the well-paying, blue-collar jobs America is in sore need of. This, in turn, can boost overall growth in the economy.

Both of these points are right. But there is a message that is missing: public health and safety, i.e., appealing to the values filter.

In our study, health, safety, and security were the top-ranking benefits compared to four other benefits, including jobs and economic competitiveness.

We've seen bridges collapse, water systems contaminated, and dams fail. But the health and safety benefits of infrastructure investment don't appear to be as prominent in messaging as things like productivity and jobs.

An opportunity for advocates of infrastructure is to go beyond the economic benefits and show how investments today can improve health, prevent accidents, and save the lives of family, friends, and their communities in the future.

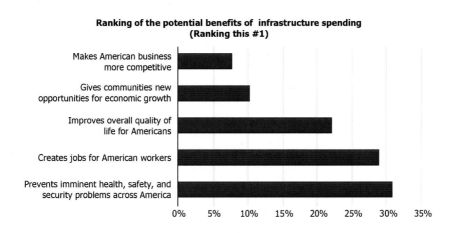

Ranking of the potential benefits of infrastructure spending (Ranking this #1)

RELEVANCE

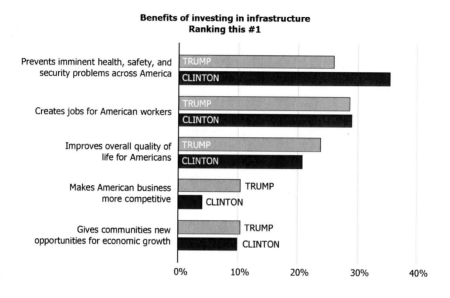

Benefits of investing in infrastructure
Ranking this #1

While the pattern of infrastructure investment benefits was largely held along political lines, there were modest differences between Trump and Clinton voters.

Clinton voters responded much stronger to health, safety, and security benefits, while Trump voters responded more positively to the benefits of improved quality of life and business competitiveness.

The BIG difference here was gender. Women were twice as likely as men to put health, safety, and security as their top benefit.

For men, jobs were the number one benefit, with security a distant second.

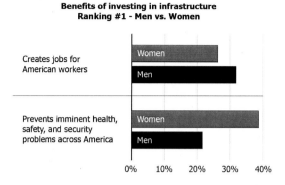

**Benefits of investing in infrastructure
Ranking #1 - Men vs. Women**

RETHINK THE CONVERSATION

Insight Number 4: There are constituencies out there for every infrastructure component.

The good news is that for every piece of the infrastructure we tested, there are "natural" constituents who recognize the need and support funding for that area.

In other words, for each infrastructure element, there are natural and logical groups who can (and should!) form the basis of a grass-roots effort to keep infrastructure at the top of every elected official's priority list.

Our study identified the top constituencies, or strongest support-ers, for each element of our infrastructure.

By targeting, engaging, and activating these constituencies, every part of our nation's infrastructure can have a proverbial voice and a proverbial seat at the table when infrastructure investments are made.

Infrastructure system	Strongest advocates (based on a mix of data)
Roads and bridges	Older (Boomers) males living in the Northeast
Drinking and waste water systems	African American and Hispanic females living in the South
Electric energy grid	Millennials (in general) along with Republicans and Independents
Urban mass transit systems	Millennials, African Americans, and Hispanics living in urban areas
Air transportation	Millennials and Gen Xers with college degrees and above-average incomes

BROADEN FUNDING AND OVERSIGHT

Insight Number 5: Spread out the risk and the rewards.

Although many inside and outside of the government agree on the need for massive spending, finding the necessary money for that spending has been a challenge.

In our study, there were mixed signals on voters' willingness to pay more taxes to improve infrastructure. The elements of infrastructure that Americans said they'd be willing to pay for aligned with their priorities. Over half said they'd pay more taxes to improve water systems (51%), followed by transportation (44%), then energy (43%). After that, there was a significant drop.

Trump voters said they were just as willing—and in some cases even more willing—to pay more in taxes for infrastructure than those who said they voted for Hillary Clinton. The biggest difference came between men and women, with women being much more frugal than men and consistently less willing to pay more in taxes for any of the infrastructure elements offered.

Our survey strongly suggests that there's no broad base of support for funding infrastructure solely by raising taxes.

We offered voters three options: fund through tax increases, fund through spending cuts, or fund through a combination of the two.

More than four-in-ten (42%) say that the infrastructure investment should come from budget cuts elsewhere. Slightly more than one-quarter (27%) say that infrastructure spend should be fully funded through tax increases. A little over thirty percent say it should be a combination of the two.

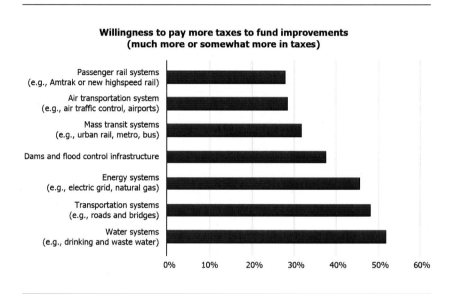

Willingness to pay more taxes to fund improvements (much more or somewhat more in taxes)

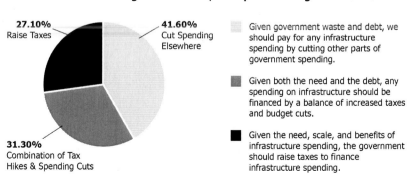

When it comes to funding infrastructure, what path should government take?

27.10% Raise Taxes

41.60% Cut Spending Elsewhere

31.30% Combination of Tax Hikes & Spending Cuts

Given government waste and debt, we should pay for any infrastructure spending by cutting other parts of government spending.

Given both the need and the debt, any spending on infrastructure should be financed by a balance of increased taxes and budget cuts.

Given the need, scale, and benefits of infrastructure spending, the government should raise taxes to finance infrastructure spending.

RELEVANCE

WHAT ALL THIS MEANS

Upgrading and modernizing our country's infrastructure is one of the biggest economic challenges facing our country today.

Our study suggests that:

1. Voters still don't fully appreciate the seriousness of the situation and severity of the infrastructure challenges we face.

2. Voters' top priorities are maintaining clean water, efficient and affordable energy, and sound transportation systems.

3. The biggest benefit voters see from infrastructure investment is improved security, health, and safety.

4. Voters want a balanced funding approach and have the greatest trust in local leaders to allocate that funding.

5. All that said, every piece of our infrastructure has a natural constituency of support.

9

What Do Americans Want From Space Companies?

For one thing, relevance to our life on Earth. The best way to provide that may be to appeal to each of our four quadrants.

Space?

Why are we writing about space? Because it is the perfect stand-in for any company, organization, or person who truly wants to go, in the words of the opening of every Star Trek adventure, where no one has gone before.

When you are creating the truly new, you need to find a way to be relevant.

Space, once the government's exclusive domain, poses the most exciting economic, scientific, and humanistic opportunities for the private sector today.

The proof is all around us. Entrepreneurs are planning:

• Constellations of satellites that promise a wealth of benefits for agriculture, education, disaster prevention, security, logistics, and commerce.

• Dramatically improved internet service, thanks to all those satellites.

• Mining of asteroids and other heavenly bodies.

• Construction of settlements on the moon—and beyond.

• Adventure tours.

• Human exploration of deep space. Destination: Mars.

Meanwhile, rockets are becoming reusable, reducing both the

RELEVANCE

cost of launching satellites, and sending experiments into orbits. And those satellites, once the size of school buses, are now small enough to hold in your hand.

As a result of all this, not surprisingly, established consumer companies with no discernible connection to space are leveraging space themes to inject energy into their brands.

And by all accounts, the U.S. government is eager for private entrepreneurs to do their thing, whether as a partner with the government or as a pioneer on their own.

> Morgan Stanley estimates that the global space economy will grow from $350 billion today to $1.1 trillion by 2040.

THE AWARENESS GAP

Given everything that we just talked about, it is odd that most Americans are disconnected from space, both the fact of it today and the enormous opportunity of tomorrow. Case in point: Our space group co-leader is often asked if he has been to the moon. (Honest.)

And the moon, some seem to think, is where the International Space Station is (if they've even given it a passing thought).

This mirrors the high-tech awareness gap of the early 1970s when consumers wondered why they would possibly ever want a computer in their homes.

The new-awareness gap is a vacuum that the most prominent space entrepreneurs—people like SpaceX's Elon Musk, Virgin Galactic's Sir Richard Branson, and Blue Origin's Jeff Bezos—are rushing to fill. They are thought leaders and storytellers.

Companies that want to thrive in their efforts to secure capital, develop technologies, and make sales would be wise to become powerful storytellers and thought leaders themselves in order to become relevant. They need to connect to a broader audience. Using the four quadrants we have talked about throughout this book would be a great place to start.

WHAT AMERICANS THINK

The first step toward thought leadership is knowing what Americans are thinking.

To get an understanding, we conducted a survey. We asked more than 600 representative Americans across the country their thoughts on space today.

We learned that they:

• See national security as the top space priority.

• Support private sector activity in space.

• Yet, they want some degree of government regulation, especially when it comes to privacy protection.

• Expect space development to benefit Earth directly.

• Think the U.S. is a leader, if not the leader, in space technology.

Let's run through those findings.

NATIONAL SECURITY

Although space-based systems promise to improve life on Earth in a variety of ways, none was more important to survey respondents than defense, the clear priority among the seven services mentioned.

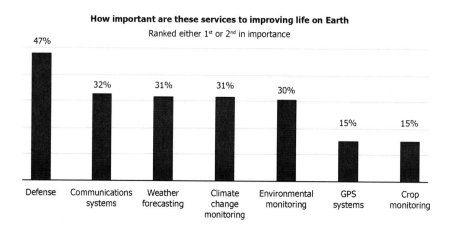

How important are these services to improving life on Earth

Ranked either 1st or 2nd in importance

47% — Defense
32% — Communications systems
31% — Weather forecasting
31% — Climate change monitoring
30% — Environmental monitoring
15% — GPS systems
15% — Crop monitoring

These findings suggest that respondents may not recognize the important role that space already plays in everyday services like GPS navigation systems (in other words, a failure to get through the rational filter). GPS systems received only 15 percent of the first and second choices, even though most consumers use them in their cars or mobile devices to get them where they need to go.

To us, this data suggests that consumers have a dated mindset—a residual impression that the space industry is primarily government-funded and intelligence-oriented—a "James Bond," Cold War view if you will.

> Many people don't realize that space already plays a role in our everyday activities.

This legacy mindset needs to be reshaped.

THE ROLE OF THE PRIVATE SECTOR

While space has historically been a government activity, Americans today prefer private over government investment in space-based activities, according to our survey.

In fact, a majority of Americans actually support private space companies receiving government incentives.

However, the support we have been talking about may come with a catch. Americans are wary of the privacy implications of flocks of satellites capturing increasingly detailed data about activities on Earth.

Strong majorities (72%) believe there should be privacy limitations on satellite companies capturing this data, and many (61%) believe that the government should have a regulatory role regarding private companies engaged in space enterprises.

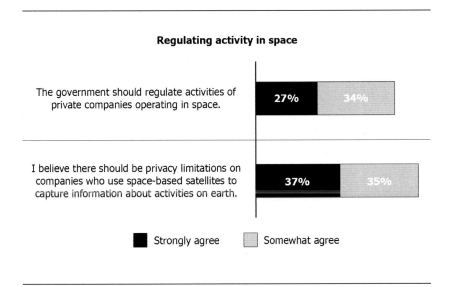

Regulating activity in space

The government should regulate activities of private companies operating in space. — 27% / 34%

I believe there should be privacy limitations on companies who use space-based satellites to capture information about activities on earth. — 37% / 35%

■ Strongly agree   ▨ Somewhat agree

EARTHLY BENEFITS

Here's the rub: Citizen support for new business activity in space may be contingent on seeing real, practical, and immediate benefits on the ground. Nearly two-thirds (65%) of Americans believe that government investments should be in those space programs that have immediate benefits to life on Earth.

On a related note, space tourism needs to make the case that it will benefit the majority of the population. Three-quarters of Americans think space travel will benefit only a few wealthy people.

Support is also tepid for government investment in deep space exploration. Less than a majority (46%) of Americans support spending government money to send a mission to Mars.

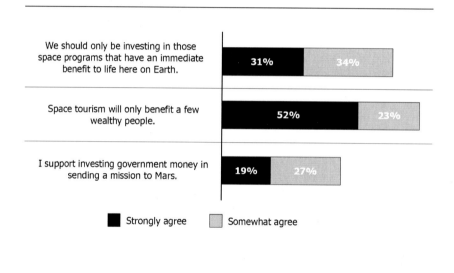

We should only be investing in those space programs that have an immediate benefit to life here on Earth. — 31% / 34%

Space tourism will only benefit a few wealthy people. — 52% / 23%

I support investing government money in sending a mission to Mars. — 19% / 27%

■ Strongly agree   ▨ Somewhat agree

GLOBAL LEADERSHIP

Finally, many Americans believe that the U.S. is a leader in space technology, with over one-third saying we are "the clear global leader." The finding represents a nice tailwind for new entrepreneurs.

Fewer respondents consider us the clear leader in energy, automotive, or environmental technology.

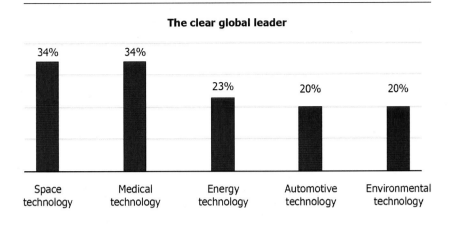

The clear global leader

But here is something important to note: Although we are perceived as a leader, Americans don't see space as terribly important to the country's competitiveness. Most people place medical technology, energy technology, and environmental technology far ahead of it.

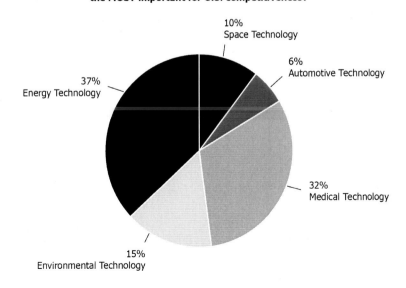

Of those technologies, which do you believe is the MOST important for U.S. competitiveness?

RELEVANCE

SUMMING UP THE RESEARCH

To recap the research: Although Americans believe we are leaders, they don't yet view space technology as critical to our national clout.

Nonetheless, there is a majority of support for the private sector in space-based activities and an openness to the government providing incentives for private companies. However, Americans will want the government to regulate space activities, particularly when it comes to privacy.

Ultimately, support for business in space may be contingent on the ability to show direct and immediate benefits to life here on Earth.

The new data provided by our research reveals a tricky communications challenge for the entrepreneurial space industry.

DEALING WITH THE CHALLENGE

Who is conquering this communication challenge today? Bezos, Branson, and Musk—not because they are great businessmen, but because they're great communicators. They have fashioned compelling stories about space exploration, tourism, and development that investors, the media, and the public are eager to hear.

They get heard today, but the industry noise is about to get louder. There will soon be thousands of companies in the new space economy, potentially drowning out one another. And as with the computer industry of the 1980s, the industry will shake out to produce winners, losers, and consolidations. As the space celebrities have shown us, success, including capital and customers, requires not only good technology but good stories well-told.

> Great companies with new technologies—and relevant stories—will thrive.

The battle for the minds of prospects, the media, and the public entails three stages of communication:

- **Awareness.** Americans today simply aren't yet tuned into space, so unless you're already a famous entrepreneur, you will need to introduce yourself and your company to the public.

- **Knowledge.** Once audiences have heard of your company, they are ready to hear the value you offer the world. Preach benefits, not features. For example, you provide real-time pictures of the Earth's surface for a variety of audiences who need them. You don't launch constellations of satellites.

- **Behavior change.** Once your key audiences know you, you need to become relevant to them. You need to ensure their perception is positive and convince them to invest in you, cover you, support you, or buy your service.

It can happen, but the industry has a lot of educating to do.

Space presents an enormous opportunity to improve human lives, expand horizons (literally), and invigorate economies.

Great companies with new technologies promise to drive this process, but they need to tell their stories well. Those who do, and who become relevant to their audiences, will thrive as the industry soars—and shakes out.

Those who don't become relevant will be left wondering why a great technology wasn't enough.

10

Simmons University

Letting the World Know You Are Something It Wants

We talk all the time about dealing with competitors, making sure our message can break through the noise and clutter in the marketplace, and the need to have a point of differentiation when we discuss marketing.

Invariably, though, we think of those things in the context of companies. How *companies* can create points of differentiation, how *companies* can deal with competition, and how *companies* can get their messages to break through to the people they are trying to reach.

But obviously, all those things apply to nonprofits, and intriguingly to colleges and universities as well. And there, the landscape is as competitive as anything you will find in the commercial marketplace.

There are 4,300 colleges and universities in the U.S. alone, and while Millennials are the largest generation that has ever lived, most of them are done with their education. While it is true that they are now having kids of their own, most of those children—the grandchildren of the Baby Boomers—won't be enrolling in a place of higher education for at least another decade.

This means there are fewer kids going to college and more competition to attract each one.

RELEVANCE

That was the situation Simmons University*—a small, selective, all-women's undergraduate college (but a co-ed graduate school) in Boston—found itself in as it entered the second decade of the 21st century.

And the school's leaders knew as the battle for students—primarily women in their case—heated up, they were at a decided disadvantage.

For one thing, research by the College Board showed that only two percent of university-bound, 18-year-old female high schoolers were even thinking about applying to an all-women's college. And for another, the school simply was not well-known outside of New England. Alumnae were proud of the school, and parents who sent their daughters there to earn an undergraduate degree were happy with the return on their investment. Still, the aggregate number of both groups was relatively small.

"I kept hearing from people who knew of Simmons that we were colleges' best-kept secret," says Cheryl E. Howard, the school's senior vice president. "When I worked in the corporate world, I was in marketing, and the last thing you wanted to hear was such and such was the best-kept secret. If you are a secret, not enough people know about you."

That anecdotal evidence about Simmons being a secret was confirmed by research that the college conducted. The people who knew of the college thought highly of it. But those who didn't said one of the reasons was there was nothing distinctive about it.

"There were no negatives, but there was nothing positive," says Howard. "It was like nothing."

This really didn't come as a surprise to Howard, who had seen firsthand that the college did not have a clear image. "When I started 11 years ago at Simmons, there wasn't a unified

*The University was founded as Simmons College in 1899 with a bequest by John Simmons, a wealthy clothing manufacturer in Boston. It became Simmons University in September of 2018.

message. Everyone had their own message that they were trying to communicate to students."

That is no way to market, especially in an extremely crowded marketplace. Something had to change.

SO, HERE'S WHERE WE START

Howard sums up the situation that the school was facing, stating, "we had done this enormous piece of research that was very insightful and very valuable, even if it was not what we wanted to hear. We were being told there wasn't a perception of what we stood for in the marketplace. That was the bad news. The good news was we felt that we had a lot to offer."

The school "just" needed to figure out how to communicate it.

As Simmons prepared to create a new approach to attracting students, leaders at the school made the decision to concentrate on promoting the undergraduate college.

"Even though our graduate program is much bigger, in terms of students," says Howard, "our president believed that universities live and die on the strength of their undergraduate reputation. So, we wanted to enhance our undergraduate reputation, and we wanted to be able to take it national."

And as senior leadership at Simmons set to work, they did have a slight head start. As part of the work it had done earlier, the college had created a firm handle on what it was and what it wanted to be and was explicitly clear about its mission, as you can see in the sidebar Who We Are.

RELEVANCE

WHO WE ARE

Our core purpose/mission:

Transformative learning that links passion with lifelong purpose.

Our core values:

We are at our best when students are first.

We prepare students for life's work.

We cross boundaries to create opportunities.

We make a collective investment in community.

Our positioning statement:

For socially-minded, career-oriented individuals who aspire to a future with purpose, Simmons is a small Boston-based university that, unlike traditional schools, transforms intellectual curiosity into meaningful life's work. This is our founding mission, our uncompromising passion, and your future.

That was good, of course, but the school needed to determine four things:

1. What it wanted to accomplish with the new positioning, i.e., what success would look like

2. Where there were opportunities in the marketplace for it to achieve its objectives

3. Which ones it would go after

4. Determine the best way to communicate the fact that Simmons was relevant to the young women—remember the focus was going to be on the undergraduate college which was all-women's—who they knew would thrive at the school

Let's take the objectives one at a time.

There were many things that the college could try to accomplish, such as appealing to older (over 24-years-old) students—a fast-growing segment of the college population—and pointing out that its undergraduate program prepared students to excel in grad school. (See Chronology of the Development of Brand Tagline and Positioning.)

But if you try to accomplish too much, you just end up diluting your efforts. So, the college decided on three objectives:

1. Build a brand position that sought first and foremost to help Simmons University recruit new students. Here's the way the university put it: "With just two percent of female high school seniors indicating an interest in single-sex education, it is critical for Simmons to offer a very strong, competitive education to these women. A transformative, single-sex education is one of the key differentiators that we have when compared with the other colleges to which our undergraduate students apply."

2. Provide a common messaging framework for Simmons leadership, faculty, students, guidance counselors, parents, friends, alumnae, and prospective students to rally around and use consistently to tell the Simmons' story both internally and externally.

3. Create an overall brand position for Simmons that resonates with each of the schools within the college (business, library science, nursing, social work) while providing a cohesive and unifying narrative supporting the undergraduate school's mission, values, and vision.

The most important one, of course, was the first: creating a brand position that would allow the college to recruit new students.

WHAT WILL THE POSITIONING BE?

Armed with goals and objectives, and with help from Brodeur Partners, the college conducted a number of focus groups on

RELEVANCE

campus and talked to faculty and staff to come up with potential positioning and taglines.

The results were four different possible approaches:

Concept Direction: Concept 1.0
Two Different Taglines – Same Body Copy

Tagline 1.1

SIMMONS:
Your Moment.
LEADERSHIP:
Your Move.

Tagline 1.2

Your Moment.
Your Move.
Your Simmons.

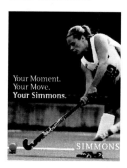

Leaders may be born. Or they may be made. But at Simmons, leaders make themselves.

You won't sit back and wait for eureka moments. You won't hope for explicit instructions to land in your lap. Rather, you'll work, discover, and evolve.

You'll learn to recognize moments of tremendous opportunity – in your career, your passion, or your life – and make the move that's right. That's leadership.

Make your move, make it count, and make Simmons your moment.

Concept Direction: Concept 2.0
Two Different Taglines – Same Body Copy

Tagline 2.1

a new
kind of
great

Tagline 2.2

DEFINE:
a new
kind of
great

Greatness: it's hard to describe, but you know it when you see it.

At Simmons, you get to define it for yourself. We start with the conviction that everyone has seeds of greatness within. Greatness can be as simple as knowing yourself and as grand as leading a global movement. Either way, it takes root when you open yourself to a wide variety of ideas, experiences, and people.

You'll cultivate your emerging greatness by exploring new depths of teamwork, creativity, global citizenship, problem-solving, and network creation. You'll emerge with profound insight into a new kind of leadership and a new kind of greatness.

Simmons: it's the place to get your great going.

RELEVANCE

Concept Direction: Concept 3.0

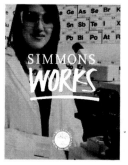

Some say higher ed is broken. That's true only when institutions lose sight of their purpose. That's why Simmons holds firm to one very visible purpose: to work for you. As an integral part of Simmons, you'll roll up your sleeves and contribute to a unique community of curious, compassionate, and ambitious people.

You'll immerse yourself in a dynamic liberal arts experience in a beacon of American culture.

Boston, you'll discover, is nothing less than your personal laboratory for experiential learning, networking, and career placement. That's just one reason Simmons works.

Another? You'll have complete freedom to mold your learning experience to your passion. And that approach has always worked.

So get ready for work at Simmons, where higher ed simply works. For you.

Concept Direction: Concept 4.0

ACHIEVE
LEAD

You don't wake up one day and declare yourself a leader any more than you declare yourself a brain surgeon. Rather, you evolve into a leader in a process fueled by self-discovery.

You explore as many ideas and experiences as you can, then focus on what truly inspires you. Next, you pursue your passions wherever they take you. They may take you to the top of the org chart, deep into the Next Big Thing, to the head of a classroom, or to foreign lands where your help is desperately needed.

Simmons is where it all comes together. It's the intersection of discovery, passion, and opportunity, the first stop on the ride of a lifetime.

Achieve, change, dream...starting right here.

"The four were tested among the prospects, both the prospective students and their parents," Howard recalls. "We were looking for the one that was most appealing and drew the broadest diverse audience, including wealthier students. We needed the wealthier students so that we could have funds to pay for students who did not have the funds to go to Simmons because at that time (2015) it cost $50,000 a year to attend as an undergraduate." (For the 2020-21 academic year, it was slightly more than $61,000.)

The testing quickly revealed that options 3 and 4 were not going to work with the target audiences. (Only 7 percent liked "Simmons Works." Just 15 percent approved of option 4, "Achieve/Lead.")

So, it was down to two.

Concept 1, as you saw, revolved around "Your Move; Your Simmons," which was seen as personal, inspiring, and easy to understand. It reflected how students thought about the process of deciding to come to Simmons. This quote is representative: "I

RELEVANCE

was deciding to make a move. It was my time to do it." People interviewed said the concept communicated that "it is all about you, and that is good." Many current students said this concept would resonate with their younger sisters or cousins.

With Concept 2, a new kind of leader, students liked the "personal narrative" of the stories about different students. The concept was seen as special—"redefining" what they are all doing right now at Simmons. "Redefining" equaled transformative in many of their minds. "At Simmons, you are the one who redefines what a leader is, what you are. It says there is the freedom to be who you are or who you want to be," was a representative quote.

CHRONOLOGY OF THE DEVELOPMENT OF BRAND TAGLINE AND POSITIONING

- March–May 2010: Core Purpose, Values, and Positioning for College developed.

- October–November 2010: Five Strategic Opportunities identified:

  o Enhancements to strengthen the undergraduate college to make it more appealing.

  o An organization-wide effort focused on creating a student-centered culture. "At Simmons, we have always valued and promoted our close connection to students. Yet this value does not always translate into everything we do. In such a competitive and increasingly impersonal marketplace, improved efforts on this opportunity will set us apart from many competitors."

  o Substantial expansion of our non-traditional undergraduate program for women over 24. "This is the largest and fastest-growing segment of potential new students."

  o Collaborative efforts—both within Simmons and externally—to articulate a wide array of flexible undergraduate to graduate school opportunities. "Students want more value and more career-readiness from their private education."

o Opportunities for online graduate education to enhance the national reach and stature of our notable schools to the overall benefit of the entire college. "In order to remain competitive, Simmons has to provide more flexible times, schedules, and learning media for our students. Online options can serve as an additional source of revenue for the college, and allow us to expand beyond our current geographic and competitive boundaries; they also allow us to sustain growth in programs where we are physically at capacity."

• September 2011–October 2012: Primary research conducted on prospective undergraduate students and their parents.

• January 2015: New tagline and positioning launched.

Many said "a new kind of" was language that resonated. It spoke to them personally and communicated, "you are different and new, and you can be whatever you want to be." It recognized that "you are an individual." One person surveyed said, "this is the perfect way to describe Simmons."

The concepts were refined a bit so that Option 1 became "Your moment. Your move. Your Simmons." And Option 2 was: "A new kind of great."

It seemed clear that Simmons had come up with two potential positioning statements that were relevant, i.e., that created an emotional connection to the target audience and would motivate them to change their behavior, i.e., get more college-age women to consider applying to Simmons as undergraduates.

The next step was to ask if both of them differentiated Simmons, i.e., to determine if other institutions were also using the keywords in their taglines. (It does you little good to use the same messaging as someone else if you are hoping to break through a crowded marketplace.)

So, was the positioning different enough?

For "Your Moment. Your Move. Your Simmons," the answer was yes; the positioning was unique. A handful of colleges used some variations of either the word "move" or "moment" (Eureka College: "The moment of discovery;" San Diego State: "Minds that move the world") but there weren't many—six in total—and none of them were even close to delivering the same message.

However, "A new kind of great," the second option being considered, was a different matter. There were 60 colleges that used the word great, and many of them did so in a context that came remarkably close to what Simmons was considering. (The University of Louisville's "Dare to be Great," and nearby University of Vermont's "The Greatness within our Grasp," and the University of Maine's "You're in a Great Place" are just three examples.)

That was a problem.

But no matter which one the school selected, it was clear that leadership, either directly or implicitly, would be part of the final message. Parents loved the idea of their daughters becoming leaders because it meant they would have a chance of landing a good job. And the research showed that the students liked the idea as well because to them, it communicated that they would be in charge of their own future.

To some, the idea that 18-year-olds would find a pitch about leadership relevant is surprising, but Howard is quick to explain why it shouldn't be.

"What doesn't resonate is to say women's leadership," Howard says. "They don't want to hear any of that stuff. But as to the concept of leadership itself, yes, it really does resonate. It's relevant.

And, of course, this is the kind of student we were looking for. So, we're looking for a student who wants to make a difference, wants to have an impact."

As they thought it through, it was clear that Option 1, with its emphasis on leadership, was the way to go.

Concept Direction: Concept 1.0
Two Different Taglines – Same Body Copy

Tagline 1.1

SIMMONS:
Your Moment.
LEADERSHIP:
Your Move.

Tagline 1.2

Your Moment.
Your Move.
Your Simmons.

Leaders may be born. Or they may be made. But at Simmons, leaders make themselves.

You won't sit back and wait for eureka moments. You won't hope for explicit instructions to land in your lap. Rather, you'll work, discover, and evolve.

You'll learn to recognize moments of tremendous opportunity – in your career, your passion, or your life – and make the move that's right. That's leadership.

Make your move, make it count, and make Simmons your moment.

RELEVANCE

"The idea that leaders make themselves was very Simmons," Howard says. "You know, it's not about you telling me what I'm gonna do as a leader. It's not about someone else saying you have to do this. It's about me developing myself and making myself into a leader. So those words resonated very well with the prospective students. We then tested the concept with our first-year students to see their responses as well, and it was also relevant. They liked the idea that you won't be sitting back and waiting for instructions. You'll seize moments of opportunity in your career, your passion, or your life."

The language was tweaked a bit, and a new subhead—stressing that Simmons is a place where leaders make themselves—was added and here is what the messaging and tag line ended up being:

YOUR MOMENT. YOUR MOVE. YOUR SIMMONS.

Where leaders make themselves.

At Simmons, we take leadership seriously. We ignore arguments about whether leaders are born or made. Because at Simmons, leaders make themselves.

Your unique leadership journey starts with an environment in which you alone define what leadership means to you and what it will take to get there. You'll draw support from students who, like you, aspire to do great things in their lives and careers. You'll experience a breakthrough new curriculum that will let you customize your desired path. You'll do it in a way that fuels you, broadens you, inspires you. You'll define your own great.

At Simmons, you won't be sitting back and waiting for instructions. Rather, you'll seize moments of enormous opportunity—in your career, your passion, or your life—and make the move that's right for you. You'll work, discover, and evolve, eventually becoming a new kind of person—still you, but with a new kind of confidence. A new kind of courage. A leader for yourself, your community, and the world. Great things await. Make your move, make it count, and make Simmons your moment.

AND WE HAVE A WINNER

The campaign was a success. You can't attribute all the recent gains at the college to one marketing decision, "but having one message that ties everything together has made a huge difference," Howard says.

Since Simmons has been using the new positioning, class size has increased—no small thing when there is a relative dearth of college-age students—and the college has become even more selective about whom it accepts. SAT and ACT scores have been increasing, and the college has become more diverse as well. Some 36 percent of those accepted to the class of 2022 identified as African American, Latina, Native American, and Asian American.

But perhaps all these gains should not be surprising when you think back to the "Relevance Egg."

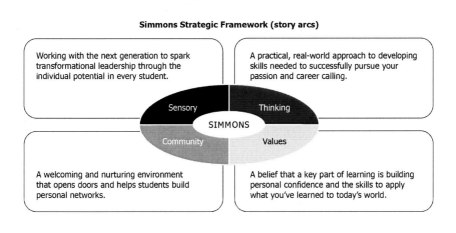

Simmons Strategic Framework (story arcs)

The new positioning resonated in all four quadrants, as you can see in the graphic above.

RELEVANCE

WHY DID IT WORK?

An intriguing question to ask, in the aftermath of the success of the campaign, is why did it work? Was the college able to find potential students who responded to the message, or did the students self-select?

"I would say it was a combination," says Howard. "Yes, we were good at finding them, using the right lists, and meeting with guidance counselors so that they would understand what Simmons is like and so they could recommend us. But we are also attracting the student leaders, the ones who are activists. The issues are so intense now with immigration, transgender issues, and the like. We are finding them, and they are finding us, students who are very caring, very activist-oriented, people who believe in equity and what is right.

"But we also have a segment of students—and I don't mean to make it sound like the two extremes—who are truly focused on their development in whatever their career is, whether it's communication, business, or nursing. They're just intensely focused on getting the most out of their education so that they have a breadth of experiences in their field.

"And then you have those who are both, activists who are very focused on their career and getting a great job or going to graduate school."

> "We used to say, 40 years ago, our role is to find this student and help her find her voice. Now we say we're looking for the student who comes in with a voice."
>
> --*Cheryl E. Howard*
> *Senior Vice President, Simmons University*

What ties this all together is the kind of student Simmons is looking for at the undergraduate level: a smart young woman who wants to accomplish something with her life. It is now clear to everyone that this is the person the undergraduate school is trying to attract.

"It's all about having something to sell," Howard says. "When I first started in admissions, honestly, we didn't have anything to sell."

They do now.

11

The Trustees' Boston Waterfront Initiative

Making Something Real: Using Relevance to Create the New

How hard could it be?

After all, who could possibly object to building a park, more specifically a world-class, "jaw-dropping park" on the Boston waterfront?

In theory, no one.

But the world does not exist in theory. And once you start talking about making such a park a reality, you understand just how much of a challenge it can be.

Let's just take the most basic decision of all—where should the park be located? Once you pick a spot—and that is no small thing, the Boston harbor comprises 50 square miles with 180 miles of shoreline—you need to acquire the land somehow. And that means someone needs to sell or gift it to you, if it is privately held, or you need to convince the government agency that owns it to turn it over to you.

Somewhere early on in that process, the people nearby have to be consulted. (Creation of a large park is going to be disruptive not only during construction but afterward as visitors come to it every day, increasing congestion and commotion in the neighborhood.)

In all, if you think about it, you have to reach seven different groups to make your park on the Boston waterfront a reality:

RELEVANCE

- Neighborhood/community organizations
- Local/state officials
- Regulatory agencies
- Businesses/developers
- The members/donors whom want this to happen. (Somebody is going to have to pay for all the work, as well as the architects, permitting, construction, maintenance, etc., required to make the park a reality.)
- Greater Boston residents, whom you are hoping to lure downtown
- Tourists/visitors you are hoping to attract

These are the challenges facing The Trustees, the nation's first and Massachusetts' largest conservation and preservation organization.

The nonprofit describes itself this way: "For more than a century, The Trustees have been on the ground in communities across Massachusetts, working to protect special places, providing loving care of our reservations, building creative new programs to engage people, and sharing our expertise with neighbors and partners across the state."

Those are noble and worthy aims, of course. But it doesn't lessen the fact that creating a massive new park on the Boston waterfront is a daunting task. And making the challenge even more difficult is the fact that The Trustees have never done anything like this before, and in fact, have never undertaken a project in Boston at all. True, they have preserved huge parts of the Massachusetts shoreline (See the Facts and Figures sidebar) and have acquired large estates and farms that have park-like qualities, but what it envisions doing in Boston would be unique for the organization, something that Matt Montgomery, the organization's chief of marketing and audience development, is quick to concede.

"We have been a fairly traditional marketing department for a nonprofit of our size," he says. "About five years ago, when I came to the organization, we transitioned from being a decentralized service shop to being a centralized strategy one. With 116 locations around the state, we had been essentially waiting to respond to requests. When I came on, we decided to build our marketing programs around the organization's priorities.

"One way we did that was through what I call a roundup model. Instead of doing marketing or promotions around one property, we would round up all of the like ideas among our properties and make it a statewide story.

"An example would be our annual Open House, where we open all of our historic houses at the beginning of the year on the same day. Leading up to it for eight weeks, we do a series of like reveals and promotions. So, by the time we get to opening day, you have been hearing about the idea for two months. And you also got reminded that we're an organization that protects a lot of places, as opposed to an organization that is just in your neighborhood or in one place. So, it helped people understand our broader impact and began to illustrate our organization, and our brand, in a different way.

"For example, we might do a roundup of 'Here are five great food experiences that you can have on our farms,' and we'll list them, and people will see they are all over the state. Now, obviously, you are only going to go to the one that is close to you. But Yankee magazine might say, 'Hey, what's this organization that does all this stuff? We've never noticed them before.' To them, one single farm-to-table place is not that interesting. But if you're an organization that produces farm-to-table dinners every weekend across five farms for 30 weekends, that is worth a feature. So, it becomes a bigger story.

"You begin to have the true impact of a big organization as

opposed to being a single place in a single community."

And the numbers bear out. Visitation to The Trustees' properties has gone from 1.2 million to 2 million in 5 years. "Our membership has gone from 42,000 households to 60,000 households," Montgomery says. "Our public programming has gone from about 130,000 participants to 250,000 in four years."

But the kind of marketing that helped the organization get there doesn't work when you are trying to build a world-class park.

In a second, we will talk about the approach The Trustees are taking to make the park a reality, but before we do, this is probably a good time to ask why they are trying to build a park in the first place.

"It comes from a couple of different perspectives within the organization," says Montgomery. "We're the largest private landowner of coastal property in Massachusetts. We've been taking care of miles of Massachusetts shoreline for years. So, we see ourselves as a steward of this coast, except we haven't been active in Boston.

"And when you think about climate change and the impact of climate change on our work, the place that you can illustrate it most easily, and see it the most clearly, is on the shoreline, because you can see the beach washing away. On Martha's Vineyard, you can literally see the sides of the island falling into the ocean and trees disappearing.

"In terms of climate change and climate impact—two things we care about—we struggled with how can we, as an organization that's just in one state, have an impact. We can educate people, but what are we educating them about? It needs to be something that we can own, and we say we know about.

"As we began to think, 'What's the most valuable, most important place that will be destroyed by climate impact in Massachusetts? The answer is Boston. And we haven't been working there. And so, we said we need to be at the table helping to bring climate resiliency to Boston.

CLIMATE RESILIENCY

What exactly is climate resiliency?

Montgomery explains.

"Along the shorelines in urban areas, you see the harbor fronts were built for industry and not to protect against rising sea tides; those structures are not going to hold as the sea rises.

"One way you can address that is with armor; you can build a wall, which we're not interested in doing. But the other way that you can do it is you can build natural environments that rebound after a storm. It's called a soft shoreline—simple things like grasses that can be washed away but will grow back. You know things will be okay when the water recedes. Those kinds of shorelines protect the city beyond.

"If your park can flood, but rebuild itself, all of the houses beyond the park don't get flooded. But if your park is a parking lot and the water just flows through it, everybody gets flooded and damaged."

"What we ultimately concluded was if we're going to make an impact, we should do what we do around the rest of the state, which is protect open space.

"Well, there's not much open space left on the waterfront, so we'll have to make it. We can create a waterfront park, but it needs to be pretty significant in order to have any kind of coastal resiliency aspect to it," he added. "So, we said, it's got to be a world-class destination park along the waterfront of Boston. Our goal now is to secure a place, make it into a world-class park, make it open to everyone, and make sure that it has a climate-resiliency benefit."

RELEVANCE

All this makes sense, of course, but the challenge for The Trustees is that the approach they took to communicate in the past won't work in trying to build a park. There are no cute animals to show, no farm-to-table events to present, no historic houses to open to bring the past alive.

And it gets harder because of all the different players involved. If The Trustees were trying to acquire a piece of land in a small town, they could meet with the neighbors, mayor, and selectmen, and it would be a fairly manageable process, one that would take a relatively short amount of time.

But "Boston is complex," Montgomery says. "You can't meet with one group and be done. You've got to meet with like 100 groups, and you're never done. And The Trustees is not known in Boston as an entity that builds parks. So, we have to introduce The Trustees to Bostonians in a way that they trust us and want us to do this work for them. And, we have to find a place so we can talk about exactly what we are trying to do.

"We're in this transition time where we need to talk about the value of open space along the waterfront without having anything concrete to point to as this is what we will do. That's a quandary from a marketing perspective."

THE INITIAL PLAN OF ATTACK

For now, given the number of constituencies they have to reach, The Trustees have decided to concentrate on just three: local and state officials, regulatory agencies, and developers.

Montgomery explains why those three.

"We need to talk to the developers before they build over all of the open space," Montgomery says. "The city and the state own the land that could potentially become a park, or they can help us with the developers. The regulatory agencies can change the purpose of some of the land.

"One of the key things about Boston to remember is that it is still a working harbor. And so, some of the areas that could be open access to the public are zoned as marine industrial, or there are regulatory restrictions over some of the places that keep them from being open space, because, for example, sometime long ago someone said: 'We have to have a place for our fishermen to unload their fish.'

"Boston is a historic reference point for building city parks because Frederick Law Olmsted was based here. He built the Boston Common and the Public Garden, which stand as examples that other cities later copied. So, there was a time when Boston was the pioneer in this area."

--Matt Montgomery
Chief of Marketing and Audience Development, The Trustees

"Well, there are not that many fishermen left. And they have more than enough space, so maybe we can change the zoning so we can build a park in the neighborhood where they use to unload their fish?

"Right now, we're focused on the people who really make the decision, who can move the project forward, or who could kill it. We need to stay in communication with them, and we need to keep working with them.

"As an organization, The Trustees is unique in that we basically build open natural spaces all over the state. That's our work, our core work, and nobody's really doing that in the city."

TALKING ABOUT THE BUSINESS DEVELOPERS

One of the requirements for the park is that it needs to be financially sustainable. "There are only a few ways you can do that," Montgomery explains. "One is, you have enough money upfront to endow it. Or it makes money on its own. You have food trucks, or you do programming, or you sell something. The third option is to say you will dramatically improve the neighborhood wherever you put your park. What if the people who benefit from that improvement pay for it?

"Well, it's hard to ask taxpayers to do that. But what if all of your neighbors for the park are corporations and they want to improve the quality of life for their employees. Or the park is surrounded by a condo project, will the developers financially support you? There is a model for this. It is similar to the cities that require a certain percentage for art. They say, 'Okay. Every new development must give a certain percent of a builder's construction project for art.' That's why you see cities like Chicago have so much great public art.

"Other cities have a requirement that you plant a certain percentage of trees for every square foot you build," Montgomery adds. "So, tradeoffs are pretty common for builders. They know in order to get their building built, they need to give a few things, and a park—or a contribution toward a park—could be one of them.

"We want to say to developers, 'work with us. We can help you understand how, if you position your building a certain way and move it back from the water, not only will it be safer, but you'll provide a little open access for people, for your employees or residents, and for the neighborhood. You'd be giving back to the neighborhood that you're building in, you'll be seen as a good neighbor, and your building lot will be more beautiful and safer.' "

And, of course, a park view can only add to the value of their development, something that is extremely appealing as well.

HOW DO YOU BECOME RELEVANT?

Objectives in place and having selected the three groups—the local and state officials, the regulatory agencies, and the developers—to target, the question becomes how do you become relevant to those groups?

"Well, the first step is understanding what they value and what motivates them," Montgomery says. "Take state and local officials. For one thing, they value what their constituencies get upset about. And they value that you talk to them first before you go public so they are not embarrassed. They value their image because it helps them get elected or re-elected. So, we value those things as well. We are not going to attack them in the press for not valuing open space. We are going to have those sorts of conversations in the privacy of their office.

"You can reach them another way, as well. We can get the public to say, 'Hey, elected officials. I value open space. As an urban dweller, my life is better if I have parks and places to recreate. My water quality is better, my air is better.' If we can do a good job of helping constituencies understand that, we can get them to tell their elected officials.

"So, you try to influence all those people—the state officials and regulators and the people they listen to. And we are fortunate there. People tend to value open space. They don't always want to pay for it, but they value it, especially urban dwellers—city dwellers hunger for outdoor space. If you've been living in Boston, then you've walked through the Common and the Public Garden and along the Greenway, so you get it. So, it's not something we have to convince you the value of. We just have to say, 'Okay. Now, you need to help us pay for it, or tell your officials to create policies that help make it possible.'"

IMMEDIATE STRATEGY

Going forward, The Trustees have a two-pronged approach for reaching its three audiences.

RELEVANCE

"Once we have a site, our communication strategy will be completely different. But up until that point, we can't talk about specific places and specific neighborhoods and specific plots of land we are considering for the park because we might jeopardize some of the sensitive conversations that are happening behind closed doors," Montgomery says. "So, the pre-designation campaign is about building brand awareness and building a value proposition to the general public and our key audiences, helping them understand why it's important, and what it can do for them.

"The objective is not only to build awareness of the initiative, but to also mobilize key players to actively support its approval. It's about changing opinion and creating an environment for action. In other words, the idea is to mobilize a grassroots movement of residents, public officials, and others to become passionate advocates for the idea of protecting the Boston waterfront from climate change and creating a world-class destination that will reshape the waterfront and the surrounding neighborhoods."

IN THE FUTURE

"Once we know where the site is, that's really when the hard work starts," Montgomery says. "Then we've got to raise the money; we've got to hire an architect; we've got to do construction; we've got to create revenue models; and we've got to get people to come and love it. And part of the process will be going through permitting and all of that. So, we'll need a lot of communications.

"Say the park ends up being in South Boston. Then we'll target the Neighborhood Association of South Boston, residents, South Boston public officials, state and local officials, and the regulatory agencies in that area and go after them with our messages as hard as we can."

But that is in the future. Today, "we're in what I call the public awareness phase. Remember, as we do this, one of our other goals is to establish our leadership in this area. So, we might begin to have social media channels where we share articles about the health benefits of open space to urban dwellers, with the idea being that people will see it and go 'Oh, The Trustees. Yeah, they're in the urban open space field. They do that.' They will begin to connect our brand with the concept of creating open space in the city.

"The other thing we will be doing is becoming more visible in Boston. We're certainly known because we have been in Massachusetts for more than 125 years. But even people who know us kind of go 'huh?' when they think of us being in Boston. We've heard that from some of our own members. They've said, "I don't understand how this is like the other work that we do."'

"I understand their questions, but I have one in return. At what point did we become an organization that conserves land in Massachusetts except for Boston? That was never our mission. I think at some point, the organization began to focus outside of Boston because it was easier, honestly. There were a lot of beautiful places all over the state, and there were owners willing to give them to us, sell it to us, or work with us. And then once we became established in a region like the North Shore or the South Shore, it was easier to do the next deal. Once you have three properties in a region, you don't have to go in and say, 'Hi, I'm from The Trustees. Let me explain to you what we do.' They often call us. So, the deals come easier.

"The other thing is Massachusetts has the second-highest penetration of regional land trusts after California. So, one thing that has happened in recent history is that smaller areas in the state have developed their own land trusts, very often modeled after The Trustees, and all of them are doing really great work, and many of them are doing the work that we used to do. So that means we should do the harder work. We should move to the next level because they can't do the complicated deals.

"So, there's been a shift in the organization's thinking. For ex-

173

ample, about 20 years ago, the organization decided that it should become a farmer because there was a crisis among farmers who couldn't afford to keep working the land. And so, we became a dairy farmer and a vegetable farmer. We adapted. We said, 'People are really interested in local food, and understanding what farmers do connects them to valuing healthy land.'

"With the Waterfront Initiative, we asked ourselves the question, 'What place is the most in jeopardy in Massachusetts?' It would be the Boston Waterfront. The ramifications of what could happen are pretty serious.

"So, it's an interesting shift for us, but it is a story that we've got to get better at telling because we've got a lot of people—both our own members, our own constituents and then the public—who don't understand it. We've got a lot of people that we need to tell the story to."

Despite the challenges, the goal with the Waterfront Initiative is totally consistent with The Trustees' mission, says its president and CEO Barbara Erickson.

"This is what we've been doing throughout our history—saving the irreplaceable."

THE TRUSTEES FACTS & FIGURES

EMPLOYEES
Full-time staff positions: 290
Part-time staff positions: 95
Seasonal staff positions: 509

MILESTONES

FIRST PROPERTY ACQUIRED
Virginia Woods, Stoneham, Mass. (20 acres, acquired 1892)

FIRST HISTORIC HOUSE PROPERTY
The William Cullen Bryant Homestead, Cummington, Mass. (1927)

LARGEST RESERVATION
Notchview, Windsor, Mass. (3,108 acres)

SMALLEST RESERVATION
Redemption Rock, Princeton (¼ acre)

FIRST TRUSTEES-HELD CONSERVATION RESTRICTION
Charles River, Sherborn (81 acres, 1972)

LARGEST TRUSTEES-HELD CONSERVATION RESTRICTION
Nashawena Island, Gosnold (1,900 acres, 1976)

LARGEST CLUSTER OF TRUSTEES-HELD CONSERVATION RESTRICTIONS
North Road, Monterey and New Marlborough, Mass. (2,396 acres)

MILES OF COASTLINE PROTECTED: 120.
The organization is the second-largest owner of waterfront property in Massachusetts. Only the federal government owns more.

TYPES OF PROPERTIES

HISTORIC HOUSES AND STRUCTURES
The Colonel John Ashley House, Sheffield, Mass.
The Eleanor Cabot Bradley Estate, Canton, Mass.
Brooks Law Office at North Common Meadow, Petersham, Mass.

The William Cullen Bryant Homestead, Cummington, Mass.

Cape Poge Lighthouse, Cape Poge Wildlife Refuge, Martha's Vineyard

Castle Hill, Ipswich, Mass.

The Inn at Castle Hill, Ipswich, Mass.

Choate House at the Crane Wildlife Refuge, Essex, Mass.

The Folly at Field Farm, Williamstown, Mass.

The Guest House at Field Farm, Williamstown, Mass.

Great Point Lighthouse, Coskata-Coatue Wildlife Refuge, Nantucket Island

The Paine House at Greenwood Farm, Ipswich, Mass.

Long Hill, Beverly, Mass.

The Mission House, Stockbridge, Mass.

Naumkeag, Stockbridge, Mass.

The Old Manse, Concord, Mass.

The Stevens-Coolidge Place, North Andover, Mass.

GARDENS

Ashintully Gardens, Tyringham, Mass.

The Eleanor Cabot Bradley Estate, Canton, Mass.

Long Hill, Beverly, Mass.

The Mission House, Stockbridge, Mass.

Mytoi, Martha's Vineyard, Mass.

Naumkeag, Stockbridge, Mass.

The Old Manse, Concord, Mass

The Stevens-Coolidge Place, North Andover, Mass.

GORGES AND WATERFALLS

Bear's Den, New Salem, Mass.

Chapelbrook, Ashfield, Mass.

Chesterfield Gorge, Chesterfield, Mass.

Doane's Falls, Royalston, Mass.

Glendale Falls, Middlefield, Mass.

Spirit Falls at Jacobs Hill, Royalston, Mass.

Royalston Falls, Royalston, Mass.

[Continued]

LARGE WOODLANDS (500 ACRES+)

Brooks Woodland Preserve and Swift River Reservation, Petersham, Mass.

Copicut Woods, Fall River, Mass.

Noanet Woodlands, Dover, Mass.

Notchview, Windsor, Mass.

Ravenswood Park, Gloucester, Mass.

Rocky Woods, Medfield, Mass.

Ward Reservation, Andover and North Andover, Mass.

Whitney and Thayer Woods, Hingham and Cohasset, Mass.

NATIVE AMERICAN HISTORY

Rock House Reservation, West Brookfield, Mass.

Pegan Hill, Dover & Natick, Mass.

Redemption Rock, Princeton, Mass.

Tantiusques, Sturbridge, Mass.

The Mission House, Stockbridge, Mass.

NATIONAL DESIGNATIONS

NATIONAL HISTORIC LANDMARK

The William Cullen Bryant Homestead, Cummington, Mass. (1966)

The Old Manse, Concord, Mass. (1966)

The Mission House, Stockbridge, Mass. (1968)

Castle Hill, Ipswich, Mass. (1998)

Naumkeag, Stockbridge, Mass. (2007)

NATIONAL REGISTER OF HISTORIC PLACES

The Colonel John Ashley House, Sheffield, Mass. (1975)

The Stevens-Coolidge Place, North Andover, Mass. (1979)

North Common Meadow, Petersham, Mass. (1982)

Tantiusques, Sturbridge, Mass. (1983)

Cape Poge Lighthouse at Cape Poge Wildlife Refuge, Martha's Vineyard (1987)

The Paine House at Greenwood Farm, Ipswich, Mass. (1990)

NATIONAL NATURAL LANDMARKS

Bartholomew's Cobble, Sheffield, Mass. (1971)

12

How Avnet Escapes
the Commodity Trap

"Let Us Help You Make Money"

There may be nothing worse for a marketer than to be seen as offering a commodity product or service.

Think about it. Suppose you run a housecleaning business. How are you going to differentiate yourself? All your competitors say—just as you are tempted to do—that they will come when they say they are going to, will get the customer's house really clean, and have a friendly, cheerful, bonded, and insured staff.

How can you possibly stand out?

Sure, you could offer to provide other services. ("We clean windows." "We will swing by your house when you're on vacation to make sure everything is okay.") Or you could say that you use only organic, non-harmful cleaning products. But others can offer all those things, too. And then you are back in the same proverbial boat and are once again seen as a commodity.

If you can't find a way out of the commodity trap, the only other option you have is to charge less—"we are the least expensive housecleaners in town"—but that really isn't a viable strategy over the long-term. For one thing, someone can always undercut you by a dollar (or a penny should it come to that), and for another, it will be extremely difficult for you to make money and sustain your business. If you compete on price, not only is it very difficult to scale, it is difficult to survive.

RELEVANCE

FROM HOUSECLEANING TO HIGH TECH

If you substitute electronics distributor for housecleaning services, you have an (oversimplified) understanding of the challenge Avnet was facing. Oh, sure. The numbers were dramatically bigger. Avnet, a Fortune 200 company, has revenues of about $20 billion a year. And the business is far more complex than house-cleaning. The company serves the aerospace and defense, automotive and transportation, communications, industrial, and security industries, among others. But the basic situation it faced really was not substantially different than the one your local house cleaner is up against.

As more and more competitors entered Avnet's marketplace offering basically the same products, the company—which started 100 years ago (in 1921)—ran the real risk of being reduced to commodity status.

At its heart, the company's challenge was determining how to adapt its marketing strategies to thrive in this new, more competitive environment.

The good news came in two flavors: The company had undergone transformations like this before, and it had a plan for this one as well.

Let's take those points one at a time, beginning with its history of transformations. Charles Avnet started the company by buying surplus radio parts and selling them to the public in lower Manhattan on "radio row" where similar companies had set up shop. As radio manufacturing grew, parts distribution took off. A few years later, when factory-made radios began to replace those constructed from various parts and kits by hand, he adjusted his distribution pipeline and began selling to manufacturers and dealers.

From there, Avnet diversified his company by branching out into car radio kits. During the Great Depression, he shifted his focus from retailing to wholesaling. And the transformations continued. By 1955, the primary business of what was then known as the Avnet Electronic Supply Co. was selling capacitors, fasteners, and switches. Today, most of the company's revenues come from electronic components, such as semiconductors.

> Market needs change quickly. Avnet has a long history of adapting to change.

As the company proudly notes on its website: "For nearly a century, Avnet has been adapting to wave after wave of technological developments to help customers, and has done so by divesting business, buying new ones, and investing in new audiences for its products."

And as for the plan for adapting, Jessica Daughetee, Avnet's Chief Marketing Officer, says it was straightforward (although, as we will see, that does not mean simple to execute).

She begins by clearing up a potential misconception.

"Electronic component distribution is still a core part of our business," she says. "It is at the heart of what we do, still. So, we're not abandoning that in any way. (See the sidebar Building on What it Had.) In fact, it's the foundation for us being able to transition. But the margins that exist in distribution are really, really, really slim.

"We needed to figure out another source of revenue that would have higher margins in order to sustain and grow the company for another hundred years," she adds. "When you see steadily declining margins, you realize there are two directions you can go. We could keep going down the same path, knowing that where we were heading wasn't good. The other option was to ask how do we transform the business, how do we leverage both the strength of who we are and our expertise, and build upon that.

"Ultimately, our job as marketers is to drive revenue," she explains. "To do that, we've got to really identify and show what it is that we can do to help our customers achieve their goals and objectives. We need to prove to them that we understand what their business needs and challenges are, and come at it from that perspective, as opposed to what we had been doing, which was explaining how great our products were and why you should buy from us."

What that meant was Avnet needed to reinvent itself and be seen differently than it had been in the past. It didn't want to be viewed as the typical electronic components distributor, but rather as a partner to those it was serving.

Says Daughetee: "We knew we had to change the narrative on how we talked about who we were; just continuing down the path of talking about parts wasn't going to get anyone to see us any differently."

In short, Avnet is positioning itself as a solutions company.

BUILDING ON WHAT IT HAD

As Daughetee explains, the shift to solution selling is just a natural evolution.

"We did a survey of our customers, partners, and employees to really understand the value that everyone sees in Avnet. What are our unique attributes? Why do people come to us?

"As we looked at those survey results, we saw one of the big unique differentiators of us versus our competitors was the relationships that we built, the partnerships we created, in trying to help guide people through a complicated buying process.

"As a result of those findings, we created a new messaging

platform about how we could serve as a guide for our customers, versus just being a transactional company. We said, 'we're going to keep focusing on how we can help you.'

"That gave us the license to ask ourselves, where could we take that positioning?

"Well, you can take that to guiding customers, not just on component distribution selection, but helping them with other parts of their business and putting together the whole picture. Because a lot of times customers have an idea on the back of a napkin, but they don't really know how to actually turn that idea into a real product."

In solution selling, Avnet is helping clients figure out exactly what they should do in creating products that will live in the world of the Internet of Things (IoT), the interconnection of computing devices embedded in everyday objects that enable them to send and receive data via the internet.

> "Shifting to solution selling is a really big change for our company, but it's a natural fit for us to grow into because it builds on the foundation of who we are."
>
> --*Jessica Daughetee*
> *Chief Marketing Officer, Avnet*

"Moving into IoT builds upon our core because the products we offer are part of IoT solutions," Daughetee says. "By being in the IoT space, we can help put together the entire solution—rather than just selling the component part of it—by helping with the initial design, prototype, the applications that are needed, the cloud service, the security, and everything else. We can put together an end-to-end solution for customers."

Daughetee gives a representable, albeit fictional, example.

RELEVANCE

"We might say to a customer, 'we understand that you are having issues with time to market, given how complex technology has become. Let us help you figure that out and get to where you need to be.'"

STEP BY STEP

The transition to solution selling is occurring in well-thought-out steps.

"One of the first things we really needed to do was create awareness that we exist in this new space because people don't know us here," Daughetee says. "We needed to explain that yes, we are a distributor, but we are now more than that, and we have these capabilities and services that you did not know we offered. That is not a job done at this point.

"From there, we have started working on establishing thought leadership in the space so that we're not seen as just another player in the Internet of Things, or whichever field where we are competing. Today, practically every company in the world is saying we do IoT. To stand out, we started contributing articles to key business, trade, and industry publications so that people could see that we really knew what we were talking about.

"For example, we have talked about 'IoT purgatory.' Practically every company knows they need an IoT strategy. And some have attempted it, but the reality is, it's so complex, and there are usually so many different partners that need to be involved in building your solution that it gets very overwhelming and very costly very quickly. We wanted to really show we understand the business challenges and point out that it is probably easier to go with one partner who has all the skills you need to build out an IoT strategy than to try to cobble it together on your own.

"So, in the thought leadership space, we focus on the things that matter to our customers. How can they reduce cost? How can they reduce the complexity of all of the technology? How do we improve their time to market so that things don't drag on?

"The last thing is really driving demand for the solutions," she adds. "And so we've started that work as well. It's going well; we're getting some good traction behind it."

DOING EVEN MORE

Not only has she been charged with helping the company's business model, Daughetee has also been tasked with creating an emotional connection with Avnet's customers, people who by trade are engineers, developers, or highly involved in the application of technology.

The idea behind trying to forge the connection is simple (and central to the concept of relevance). If all you have is a transactional relationship with a customer, they have no real loyalty to you. They will leave without a second thought if they can get a superior deal (better terms, quicker delivery, a lower price, etc.) If you are in a purely transactional relationship, you are basically back to commodity status.

Daughetee needed to help change that.

Here's how she explains what she has done.

RELEVANCE

AVNET AND RELEVANCE

Where does relevance fit in all this?

"To me, the concept of relevance was a great way to re-look at our business and make sure we were hitting all the key things to make sure that we were talking to our customers in a way that matters to them. That we are showing them that we want to understand and meet their business needs versus just putting out what we want to say about our business," Daughetee explains. "I think stressing relevance was a great reminder. Sometimes, you get caught up in, 'here's what we want to communicate.' Relevance makes us say, 'hey, don't forget. It's really not about what you want to put out there; it's what your customers need and want.'"

"I don't know that it's brain surgery, but we started by saying no matter how technical the audiences, they're still people," Daughetee explains. "That means they care about the same things everyone else cares about. So, we are coming at it from a perspective of how can we connect with them emotionally? How can we show how what we're doing is making an impact on the world? Or can make an impact on what they're doing in their business.

"Instead of making them sort through messages about who we are and what we offer, we talk about what we can do for them, and the impact our products have had on other customers.

"That has created a new level of engagement, and it has opened up new types of audiences for us. Typically, people think of us in a very specific way. We're very B-to-B; that's how we've been known; we're very supply-chain-distribution-oriented. But by going to market and talking about how we're helping prevent SIDS and helping parents get a good night's rest through a product like the Happiest Baby's SNOO bassinet (which keeps a baby on their back while they sleep and automatically jiggles and sends out white noise when a baby begins to fuss), they see us differently. (Avnet provided engineering design support in the creation of the product and handles logistics for rental customers.)

"Taking this approach suddenly opens up all kinds of additional markets, people we call non-traditional customers. Companies that historically wouldn't have thought to work with us go, 'Wow, they helped this company that is creating baby cribs? Maybe they could help us,'" Daughetee adds. "This approach was really about making us relevant with a new audience, as well as changing how we were perceived by our existing customers so that they would look beyond just working with us for products and then going to other companies for the solutions and services that we offer. It was a big effort to try to get our existing customers to think of us differently.

> "Telling more emotional and compelling stories that show we're impacting different types of businesses is helping us not only connect with our target customers, but is allowing us to connect to a broader audience as well, companies we have not previously worked with."
>
> *--Jessica Daughetee, Chief Marketing Officer, Avnet*

"Before, we were very product-centered. 'Buy this sensor because this is what it does.' And we did the vast, vast majority of our marketing through our suppliers. Now we've really moved to solutions selling and storytelling. 'Hey, you've got issues in your business where you don't have the visibility you need into what's happening with your tools; we can help because if something goes down, you're down for a long time, and it impacts your bottom line.'

"As a result of our shift in marketing, we can go out and tell stories about predictive maintenance and tell stories about Avnet and what Avnet is doing to help with that. (See sidebar: How Solution Selling Plays Out in Practice.) Products are a part of that, but it's not the whole part of that. We can help show customers the bigger picture.

HOW SOLUTION SELLING PLAYS OUT IN PRACTICE

Sure, you could sell individual component parts to the world's largest coffee retailer, but wouldn't being a true partner be better?

Avnet answered that question with a yes. Working with the coffee company, it created predictive maintenance solutions that reduce and eliminate downtime.

"With this solution, which employs the sensors Avnet sells, you can do active maintenance," Daughetee says. "You can ensure that your baristas aren't waiting around for their coffee makers to be fixed because the system will predict when a part is going to go bad. That allows you to fix it ahead of time.

"Before, Avnet wouldn't have been involved directly with the coffee company at all," she adds. "We would have sold our sensors to another company which would have built a solution for the retailer.

"So, what's really changed is we are now working directly with the end-user—the companies that actually use our product, instead of a middle man—and saying let's figure out what you want the final outcome to be. In the case of the coffee retailer, it was to eliminate downtime. Then, once we know the goal, we can talk about how we can get you there," Daughetee explains.

"The components are certainly a part of that. What components do we need to build into the solution in order to accomplish the goal? But we also layer on the software. And the services. We add in all those things in order to give them the full solution versus just selling components to somebody else who they buy their solution from."

This approach, of course, boosts revenues and earnings. But it also does something else. It forges a closer relationship with the end-user, making it easier to sell more to them going forward.

"We are offering solutions, stressing the end-user benefit, as opposed to saying 'If you're creating something that needs a sensor, buy this sensor,'" Daughetee says. "We're still selling sensors, but we're also selling solutions and services."

WHAT DOES IT TAKE TO MAKE THIS WORK?

Selling solutions is a rational way to position Avnet's marketing evolution. However, you still need emotional components, buy-in internally, and acceptance from customers that you are the right organization to use this approach.

Let's deal with all three factors, starting with the emotional components.

"I think trust, credibility, and authenticity were really important for us in making the transition," Daughetee says. "We had to get people to believe we could expand successfully into these new areas, that we could be trusted, and we were a credible source of information or expertise in these new areas. And so, thought leadership, for example, was a big part of what we focused on to start. We established ourselves as experts and as a trusted source in the places where we wanted to compete."

As for getting everyone aboard, "it was pretty hard at first to sell it internally," Daughetee concedes. "The company had a very traditional approach from a marketing perspective. I think they thought of what we were doing as marketing fluff. They didn't see the value of what it delivered to the company. So, from an internal perspective, I think it was an uphill battle. Bringing in results was the number-one thing that started to get them thinking differently.

"The number-two thing, quite honestly, is we had a regime change, we had a new C-suite move into the company, and the new leadership knew the world of marketing, believed in marketing and its benefit. And they really believed that marketing was critical to shifting how the company was perceived. So, when that happened, there was much more support internally to get behind what we were doing. I'm not going to lie; the change in leadership helped a lot."

And customer buy-in?

"It's been a journey," Daughetee says. "At first, they didn't understand it. So it took a lot of education as we were acquiring companies and trying to help them understand how building out this broader ecosystem would benefit them.

"It was a heavy lift for a long time and we're still going through that. But the idea has now got momentum, and it's built, and built, and built. We've put so much energy and effort behind these new areas of the business that customers are now like, 'Okay, we get it. How do we get involved? How do we become part of this bigger thing you're doing, instead of this transactional stuff that we've been doing with you up to now?'

"But, as I said, it was definitely a heavy lift, especially trying to help them understand why we acquired Hackster.io and Farnell and its element14 unit. They asked, 'Why would you buy that? What is that doing for us?'"

But there are now more than one million people who are members of Avnet's online communities, element14.com and Hackster.io, creating the world's largest collaborative network of engineers, entrepreneurs, and developers who learn from each other's ideas. element14 and Hackster help product developers all over the world get work done faster and more effectively. Instead of scouring several sources for answers, members turn to the Avnet communities for consolidated information on new technologies, as well as access to experts.

> "It's really about understanding and identifying the challenges of our customers and figuring out how can we help solve for those and ultimately then drive business for our company."
>
> *--Jessica Daughetee, Chief Marketing Officer, Avnet*

"What we explain is by having these communities, we can help our customers put their products in front of developers at the very, very early stages as those developers start building out their solutions." The thought being that the developers will use Avnet's customers' products in the ones they are developing.

As Daughetee says, "The online communities are a great resource. You can discover what the developers think about X, Y, or Z. Or how they might approach a particular problem. Or you could throw out a challenge of 'What would you do with this product? What's the most creative thing you could do with this sensor?' It took a while for some of our customers to understand that."

GOING FORWARD

"I think we are finally on a path where we're looking ahead, we're looking at the trends, we're looking at what's happening in technology, and we're participating in those conversations far earlier," Daughetee says.

"We used to be very inward-focused or focused on our suppliers and our customers. We still are focused on them, of course. But now we recognize and see the importance of being involved at a higher level and entering into conversations about the future of 5G, the future of robotic process automation, or artificial intelligence. We are really inserting ourselves into those conversations very early on to establish expertise and credibility.

RELEVANCE

And that's something we're going to continue to do—we're going to be looking at what's coming and asking how do we get associated with it at the outset.

"We always say, as a hundred-year-old company, we've had to adapt to wave after wave of technological change. And that's true. But in the past, often we've been behind in getting there, and we play catch up every time one of those changes happen. And I think for the first time ever, we're now in a place where we're absolutely looking ahead and trying to establish our presence and our relevance in those spaces very early. That way, when those trends mature, we become a known factor and leader in the space, a company that people naturally would want to go to."

13

Hankook

Making Sure You're Seen as Unique

In the last chapter, we discussed the (successful) steps Avnet, the global electronic components distributor, is taking to avoid being seen as a commodity supplier.

But what do you do when most people already see you as a commodity? How can you differentiate yourself?

That is the challenge Hankook Tire America Corp., the Nashville-based subsidiary of Hankook & Company Co., Ltd. group of South Korea ($5.9 billion in revenues), is facing as it tries to grow sales in the United States. On its face, there is nothing distinctive about either the company or its tires. While the parent company is one of the world's largest tire companies—it is now seventh globally—that in and of itself is not distinctive. (It means you are big, but you are not the biggest.)

And the company certainly does make good tires. But this sort of review is representative:

"Hankook is the second-most affordable tire brand among the top tire brands, and the company has good options for sedans and truck sizes," reads a report from Top 10 Reviews, a digital publisher. "Hankook emerged [in our review of the entire United States tire industry] as an affordable tire brand with the best tread-life warranties available."

Again, it is far from a pan, and "best tread-life warranties" is something you can point to, but it is not the sort of rave that makes

RELEVANCE

your brand stand out.

The parent company proudly boasts of its 80-year history—founded in 1941, it was the first automobile tire company in Korea—but in reality, as you know, people don't give you a lot of credit for your corporate history. It makes them feel better that you are probably going to be around if anything goes wrong, but other than that, it really isn't a differentiator. (And even if it were, Hankook's largest competitors have been around far longer. For example, Michelin was founded in 1889, Goodyear in 1898, and Bridgestone in 1931.)

So, how do you create relevance around a tire, especially when you are selling a Korean-branded tire in the United States, a market dominated by American brands? (True, in 2017, Hankook opened a plant in Clarksville, Tennessee that can turn out 5.5 million tires a year, but most people don't know that.)

How do you become relevant?

The question of relevance is of particular importance since Hankook is in the midst of trying to gain significant market share in the U.S. where it has around 4 percent of the U.S. replacement tire market (passenger and light truck). That puts Hankook among a half dozen or so brands with similar share competing to chip away at the big three–Goodyear, Michelin, and Bridgestone. So, where do you begin to create relevance?

It is a two-step approach:

1. You start by figuring out which segment of the driving public to go after.

2. Then you use the Relevance Egg as one of the ways to determine the best way to reach them.

Let's deal with the target market first.

BABY YOU CAN DRIVE MY CAR

Hankook decided to concentrate on men between 25 and 54 years old, which makes sense. Far and away, that age group as a whole buys the most cars and trucks (both of which need replacement tires), and within the cohort itself, the group skews male (57% to 43%), according to Hedges and Company, an Ohio-based marketing firm.

Once that decision was made, it was onto figuring out how to reach those men. And this is where the Relevance Egg proved valuable.

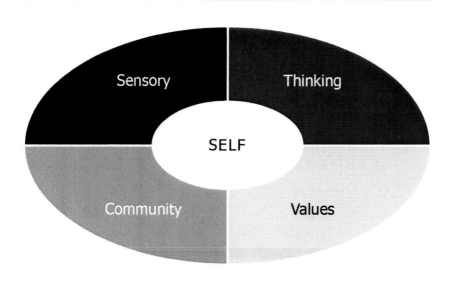

"I used to think of relevance almost in the same terms as brand awareness, but it's so much more than that," says Abby Campbell, Hankook Brand Communications Specialist. "After going through the relevance methodology and approach, I was able to understand the importance of forming a true connection with an audience in order to reach and retain them.

RELEVANCE

> "People are not always going to purchase our tires just because we make a good quality product, which of course we do. Our quality is great. But we need to do more. We have to make a connection with customers and the people we would like to be our customers."
>
> *--Abby Campbell*
> *Brand Communications Specialist, Hankook*

"It made perfect sense to me," she adds, "because when I think about why I choose the brands that I choose, I always make my decision based not only on the quality of the product or the trustworthiness of the brand, but I have a tendency to lean towards brands that I relate to on a personal level. For example, if the brand is nostalgic for me—like something my mom used when I was a kid—it reminds me of my childhood and makes me feel happy and comfortable, and I'm more likely to buy it because of that nostalgic, personal connection. Or, if the brand has an ad that is relatable and makes me think 'Oh, I do this too!' or 'I also have this problem!' then I'm more likely to purchase the product.

"That's why I think influencer marketing (a form of social media marketing involving endorsements and product placements from people and organizations who have an expert level of knowledge or are admired in their field) is so effective. Because people follow influencers that they relate to. And if an influencer is vouching for a brand, and I relate to that influencer, that must mean that I am also likely to enjoy the brand," Campbell explains.

"I've always known that it's important to resonate with your audience, but I think in the past, I would have placed brand awareness above relevance," she adds. "I used to think it was more important to have your brand name heard than it was to relate to your audience. But I've come to realize that we can't just throw out any message and expect it to achieve results. Because if a person does not perceive your message or your brand as relevant, it will fall on deaf ears."

That, of course, has been our premise throughout.

BUT HOW DO YOU REACH THEM?

So, being relevant was going to be important. But how should Hankook try to reach the men it had decided would be their core audience?

When people begin looking for connections to relevance, they usually start with the rational—the "thinking" part of the Relevance Egg, which, of course, is fine. From Hankook's perspective, the easiest way to do it would be to say its tires are of higher quality and safer. But there are two problems with that.

"First, it's a legal issue," says Campbell. "Since our tires haven't been tested against every single brand, we can't legally make the claim that our tires are safer or higher quality than others. We do speak about our quality because our tires are of top quality, but if that's all we said, then we'd just be saying the same thing that our competitors are because they make high-quality tires, too."

> "I think our biggest challenge has been trying to set ourselves apart from those competitors who are saying the same thing."
> --Abby Campbell
> *Brand Communications Specialist, Hankook*

And indeed, Hankook's previous approach to marketing had been the same as what every company was doing as well. The message could be boiled down to: "You want a safe tire to protect your family. That's what we offer." There was nothing wrong with that. But if your message is the same as everyone else's, it doesn't stand out, and if it doesn't stand out, it is difficult to be heard.

As Campbell points out, something had to change.

"If we didn't reevaluate our brand strategy, we would be at risk of falling behind our competitors, just as any other brand would," she says. "I think it's important for all brands to continuously research their audiences and evaluate their strategies to determine what is or isn't working and make the necessary adjustments. In this age of information, things change rapidly, so it's important for us to keep up if we want to gain and keep the attention of our audience.

"For us, our end goal is always to influence a purchase decision, so if we remain stagnant in our marketing efforts and don't seek to understand our end-users, we won't be able to effectively achieve that goal," Campbell adds.

Specifically, through its marketing and advertising efforts, Hankook seeks to increase brand awareness, increase brand preference, and influence purchase intent. (We will return to this idea a bit later in the chapter.)

"Over the past four to five years, our position in brand awareness and brand preference, compared to other brands, has remained virtually unchanged," Campbell says. "And of course, our goal is to surpass our competitors, so while we didn't slip in the rankings, we also didn't climb."

To improve, a new messaging approach was called for. In thinking about the best way to engage Hankook's core audience, the company decided to employ two parts of the Relevance Egg: Use the rational approach (which as you recall is this: "This product/service helps me meet my needs," and "It makes my life easier.") and combine it with the sensory (as you remember, the sensory part of the Relevance Egg is this: "This product/service is part of my routine or habit," and "It just feels right." The important part here.)

The goal was to build on and extend the "driving emotion" tagline central to its advertising.

"Driving emotion is an expression that is very close to the heart for all of us at Hankook," the company explains on its website. "It embodies everything that the company is about, and elaborately depicts what a driver deserves: a dynamic range of emotions that enable them to enjoy driving. Driving emotion stands for real driving pleasure which arises from the inseparable unit of driver, vehicle, and optimum tires."

In creating that messaging, Hankook was playing back to its target audience what it was hearing from them.

"From what I have observed on social media and through social listening, it seems people are a fan of our tires because they are good quality and they're mostly performance tires," Campbell says. "Usually the people who buy our tires are people who enjoy driving. Cars are a hobby for them. They don't just want to go and pick up any tire. They want to make sure that it's one that can add to their vehicle performance. They love to drive and are passionate about it." It is interesting to note that the parent company expanded on that insight in its marketing in Europe and Latin America, creating the "Be One with It" campaign.

Here's an excerpt from its messaging:

RELEVANCE

"Whether going to work early in the morning, coming home from work with the sunset in the background, taking your child to school, or taking a trip, driving is a huge part of our lives. At these times, the driver becomes one with the car and the outside scenery drifts by as if in slow motion. When the driver becomes completely one with the car, the true pleasure of driving can be discovered.

"From the moment a base jumper steps off a cliff wearing a wingsuit, a surfer rides a wave on a surfboard, or a snowboarder glides down a snow-covered mountain, the one common element lies in putting complete trust in their equipment to experience that extreme thrill they're seeking.

"For the ultimate driving experience and to find that perfect moment when the driver becomes one with the tires, Hankook is forging ahead with a multifaceted approach. Although it might not be easy, our goal is to do our utmost so that all drivers can discover that perfect moment."

"We have realized it is very important to make an emotional connection," Campbell says, adding that the company is trying numerous ways to do so.

"A main focus lately has been trying to reach end-users through social media, because that is where the younger audience is," Campbell says. "While we utilize traditional media—we run TV commercials and digital ads, of course, and earned PR—but we've really been pushing social media to reach that younger audience."

And the company is doing it through sponsorships as well.

"We've been reaching out to the baseball-loving audience to create that connection with them. If they love baseball, we hope that they can connect with us because we are a sponsor of professional baseball. That will drive awareness and, hopefully, sales. People often associate baseball with good memories and times with family and friends. Our hope is to have that association between good times, baseball, and the American pastime, extend to Hankook."

And, of course, you can tie that emotional connection to social media campaigns. "We've looked at doing campaigns that follow families who are getting ready to go on a road trip to see a baseball game. We discussed the idea of doing a video series that follows the families and demonstrates how they prepare for the road trip, what they pack in their car, and document their journey. You have to be creative when showing that emotional connection between tires and baseball. But I think it can be done."

And you can find other ways to connect as well. It can be as simple as price.

"In the past, younger audiences usually wanted to buy the cheapest tire in the store, but now I think that Millennials care more about the quality of the product. They want better quality," Campbell says. "It's not just about buying the cheapest thing anymore. That is working to our advantage because we're a great option. We are below the price point of other top manufacturers, so we are in an attractive price point for that audience."

BEING AUTHENTIC

Now for any of this to work, you have to remain authentic. Your message, or your influencers, can't be a stretch because if you look superficial or too promotional, people will lose interest quickly.

"We see so many influencers today on social media that come across as obvious or inauthentic. Essentially, when you see it, you can tell that it's an ad. You can tell they're just doing it because they're being paid for it, and that's what we want to stay away from." Campbell says. "When we are looking for influencers, we make sure they are fans of the brand already. People tag us in content all the time on Instagram, and a lot of them have tons of followers. If we see that someone's already a fan, we can reach out to them and see if they want to be a partner. The answer is usually yes since they already have our tires and already like the tires. That keeps it authentic because it's something they already like."

HOW IS IT GOING SO FAR?

Campbell says Hankook has three immediate goals:

• Increase brand awareness.

• Increase brand preference.

• Influence purchase intent.

"We not only want to be a well-known brand, but we want to be viewed and recognized as a top-tier, premium brand in the American market," she says. "Since we opened our first U.S. plant in 2017, our immediate goal has been to increase the awareness that we are producing premium tires in America for American consumers. So, success there would mean that we are seeing more conversations around Hankook in the media as well as see increased brand awareness results in our bi-annual brand competitiveness study.

"Success in increased preference for our brand would mean that consumers are requesting our tires rather than relying on a dealer to recommend a brand for them. They would prefer Hankook over other brands. I think success here would also mean a higher following on social media. Consumers at this stage would be more invested in our brand and want to follow us.

"Finally, if we succeed in influencing purchase decisions, that would mean increased sales. Success at this stage would mean that we have increased our number of OEM (original equipment manufacturer) partnerships while also selling more tires to end-users who specifically choose our brand over another."

While the Hankook relevance campaign remains a work in progress, the initial responses have been promising.

"From a social media perspective, we have seen an increase in followers and have received great responses from our campaigns," Campbell says. "While our social advertising budgets did not increase, our engagement rates have sky-rocketed, nearly doubling, and I think it's largely due to our creative storytelling and relatable campaigns. We've created campaigns that are of higher quality, highly engaging, and had relatable narratives. We don't want to just talk about our products; we want to show people how our products can be used to enrich their lives."

She provides two quick examples.

"We partnered with a local Tennessee band and gave them a set of tires for their tour bus and asked them to document their summer tour on Hankook tires. That really resonated with a different lifestyle audience that is a bit harder for us to reach. With our American headquarters being located in Tennessee, this also helped us draw a connection with our 'hometown Tennessee' audience and displayed our product in a lighthearted and inspiring way through the lens of a rock and roll band.

"We also built a campaign around the 'Van Life' movement, where we followed several individuals and families who travel to beautiful locations all over the country and live out of their (very 'tricked out') vans. It helped us tell an emotional brand story in a unique way while reaching an 'adventure-loving' and outdoors audience to market our new all-terrain product.

"You can see the payoff in the fact that Hankook gained followers on social media, which I think is evidence that brand awareness and preference is on the rise."

We will give Campbell the last word. While she is speaking about her company, her words could apply to every firm.

"Being a tire company, it can be a stretch at times to keep things fresh and creative to hold the attention of our audience. It's also challenging since there are so many competitors out there making the same product. That's where I think relevance comes in. One of the main ways we can increase preference for our brand is to increase our relevance in the eyes of consumers so that they'll go into their local tire shops and request our tires instead of our competitors.

"Yes, everybody needs tires, so what will make them choose ours? If we can find a way for our customers to identify with our brand on a deeper level, I think they'll be more likely to keep choosing us in the future."

14

Samsonite

Socially Relevant

We all want to have purpose in our lives and to believe in the brands we buy, work for, or invest in.

Most of us had a lot of time to think during the global pandemic caused by COVID-19. We thought about our health, of course, and keeping our families, friends, and loved ones safe. And a great many of us also pondered what is truly important to us, as we spent our days in virtual lockdown, in a new world where it was hard to separate one day from another.

A good number of us came to the conclusion that we wanted to be better people going forward. You saw that in many ways. For example, despite the economic downturn of 2020—which caused record unemployment and devastated entire industries such as restaurants, airlines, and hotels—most people who contribute to worthy causes said they planned to maintain, or even increase, the amount they donated according to Fidelity Charitable, which has become the largest grantmaker in the country by managing thousands of individual donor-advised funds. A quarter of donors planned to increase their giving in response to the hardships caused worldwide by COVID-19. Another 54 percent said they would maintain their level of charitable gifting despite all the problems in the economy.

Those were the overall figures. Younger generations planned to step up their donations in even greater numbers. Some 46 percent of Millennials —that's nearly half—said they would be giving more than they had in the year before, even though research showed that young people were hit disproportionately harder than any other cohort by the downturn.

What Fidelity Charitable found was confirmed elsewhere. For example, The New York Times reported that a study of 32 foundations, which manage charitable accounts directed at a specific city or region, showed an 80 percent increase in donations from March to May of 2020 during the early days of the pandemic, compared with the same period the previous year. The study was conducted by the Community Foundation Public Awareness Initiative.

This desire to do better, in turn, gave a turbo boost to two trends already underway. The first is the Environmental, Social, and Governance movement. ESG refers to the three central factors in measuring the sustainability and societal impact of an investment in a company or business. These criteria go beyond the financials to give a more complete picture of a firm to people thinking of working for, investing in, or doing business with an organization.

And the second movement is usually referred to as Corporate Social Responsibility (CSR), where businesses engage in and support ethically-oriented practices.

For Samsonite, the global luggage manufacturer and retailer, both trends—ESG and CSR—fit naturally into what the company has always believed. Here's how CEO Kyle Francis Gendreau put it in his message explaining the company's position on sustainability:

"The world today looks very different from when our founder, Jesse Shwayder, started a small trunk manufacturing company in Denver, Colorado, back in 1910. People are increasingly concerned about climate change and the future of our planet. More and more consumers are making purchasing decisions based not only on their taste and budget but also on sustainability credentials, including environmental impacts.

COMPANY FACTS

Samsonite, a $3.5 billion-plus luggage manufacturer and retailer with about 14,500 employees, owns the Samsonite, eBags, Speck, Tumi, Hartmann, American Tourister, Lipault, Gregory, and High Sierra brands. The publicly held company (listed on the Hong Kong Stock Exchange) makes products ranging from large suitcases to small toiletry bags to briefcases.

The company has more than 1,300 company-owned stores in 40 countries, as well as a variety of wholesale distribution channels and retail websites. It has three primary manufacturing sites in Belgium, Hungary, and India, as well as a small site in Mexico and 19 distribution centers worldwide.

"We have charted a path to lead the industry—not only in innovation, quality, and durability—but also in sustainability," Gendreau continues. "We commit to increasing the use of the most sustainable materials, models, and methods to create our products and will encourage good practices and positive impacts in our supply chain. We are also committed to taking action on carbon. As well as continuing to design products that last, we are also committed to increasing the use of recycled materials, reducing our impact on the planet.

"Building on our enduring values and our heritage of innovation, quality, and durability, we are now setting out our vision to become the most sustainable lifestyle bag and travel luggage company in the world."

In large part, it is up to Christine Riley Miller, Samsonite's global director of sustainability, to make that happen.

RELEVANCE

"Samsonite has been proud to lead the industry in innovation, quality, and durability for 110 years, and we expect to also lead in sustainability," she says about her task ahead. "The objective of the 'Our Responsible Journey' campaign, the name of our sustainability strategy, which was launched in March 2020, is to reach specific stakeholder groups with this message."

RELEVANT HISTORY

You can better understand Samsonite's commitment to sustainability, if you know that its founder, Jesse Shwayder, had the company's ethos written on a marble that was given to every employee.

You'll recognize the message. It's the Golden Rule: "Do unto others as you would have them do unto you."

As the company notes on its website, "more than a hundred years on, it remains our guiding principle for how we treat each other but also how we care for the world we live in."

Here's a bit of the company's 110 year-plus history:

1910: Shwayder, whose family owned a furniture store where he worked as a teenager, founded the Shwayder Trunk Manufacturing Company in Denver, Colorado.

1941: The company introduces a suitcase covered with sturdy vulcanized fiber dubbed "Samsonite." Shwayder explained that he sought a name that would represent the strength and durability of his new cases and chose the Biblical giant Samson to express these core values.

1956: They begin retailing Ultralite cases, the first to forego wooden box construction in favor of a revolutionary combination of "jet age" magnesium and injection-molded vinyl cellulose.

The company begins producing wheeled suitcases. The design with small wheels at the back set the standard for decades to come. (When was the last time you saw a suitcase without wheels?)

Samsonite

1965: The company changes its name to Samsonite.

1970: Shwayder, who served as company president from 1910 to 1960 before becoming company chairman, dies. At the time of his death, the company was the world's largest luggage manufacturer (and remains so).

2017: Samsonite acquires eBags, the market-leading e-commerce platform for luggage and backpacks in the U.S.

2018: The company launches Recyclex™, an innovative fabric made from 100 percent postconsumer recycled plastic bottles.

"Our ESG report and corporate website are targeted to investors primarily and employees secondarily and are intended to provide a comprehensive yet succinct summary of our ESG efforts over the previous year," she adds. "The brand websites and product marketing materials are targeted to consumers and intended to raise awareness about Samsonite's efforts to more sustainable materials in our products.

"As expectations of corporate ESG commitments continue to rise among key stakeholders," Miller says, "it's increasingly important for Samsonite to continue to communicate our efforts to lead the industry in sustainability."

> "As the world's largest lifestyle bag and travel luggage company, we are continually on a journey, growing our business, and ensuring we work with integrity at every step of the way. Our destination is to be the most sustainable lifestyle bag and travel luggage business on the planet."
>
> *--Christine Riley Miller*
> *Global Director of Sustainability, Samsonite*

RELEVANCE

Samsonite's immediate goal for Our Responsible Journey is to continue communicating its efforts to consumers, employees, and investors, Miller adds. (See sidebar: Who Samsonite is Trying to Reach.) "Success would be that these stakeholder audiences would recognize Samsonite as the industry leader in sustainability.

WHO SAMSONITE IS TRYING TO REACH

Even before launching its Our Responsible Journey, Samsonite had an obligation to share its ESG efforts with its shareholders as a requirement of being listed on the Hong Kong Stock Exchange. "So that was, and continues to be, a key stakeholder for us," Miller says.

There are two other stakeholders, as well as another group the company is trying to reach. Stakeholders first.

"Consumers are increasingly interested in what companies are doing to have a positive impact on people and the planet," Miller says. "So even early on, when the company didn't have a full strategy in place, we wanted to be able to say, 'Hey, we're starting this process. We have these great products. You can feel good about buying our products and these particular collections because there is this sustainable element to them.'"

Then there were employees who were, and are, engaged in all of the company's ESG efforts. (We will talk more about this in the "People" portion of Samsonite's sustainability platform.)

And finally, there was the media, "which became a new audience for us," said Miller.

"The intermediate goal is to develop more concrete action plans and then to establish interim milestones for achieving them," Miller says. "While it was true that Samsonite had always paid attention to its global environment and social footprint, prior to the development of Our Responsible Journey, the company did not have a formal framework or goals against which to develop action plans and demonstrate progress against our most material issues.

"With the introduction of Our Responsible Journey, the organization is aligned on four key pillars and the global goals, and collectively, we can now work toward prioritizing resources against accomplishing those objectives," she says.

PUTTING THE SUSTAINABILITY PLATFORM INTO ACTION

Samsonite's Responsible Journey focuses on four key areas important to its business: product innovation, carbon action, a thriving supply chain, and its people.

"The four areas are underpinned by specific targets which were developed after a thorough process of consultation with our internal and external stakeholders," Miller says.

Let's run through each of them quickly.

1) PRODUCT INNOVATION

The goal is simple—and ambitious. Samsonite's objective is to create "the best products using the most sustainable and innovative materials, methods, and models." The company is committed to increasing its use of sustainable materials in its products and packaging to lessen its impact on the environment.

"Redesigning packaging is a big focus for us," says Patrick Kwan, Samsonite's senior director, Supply Chain Asia. "While we must always ensure that our products arrive to the consumer in perfect condition, we've taken steps to use less packaging and switch to more sustainable materials. For example, in Asia, we've replaced Styrofoam, which can't easily be recycled, with folded cardboard, and use recyclable paper tape to seal our boxes, so our packaging is 100 percent recyclable."

Here are a couple of simple examples from the company's

RELEVANCE

ESG report of the ways Samsonite keeps the environment in mind in its manufacturing process.

The company has reduced the use of virgin zinc by 30 percent in the hardware in its TUMI bags, replacing it with recycled zinc. "This reduces the negative effects of mining, protects the depletion of this precious mineral, and decreases water and energy consumption used to extract and process zinc," the company noted in its 2019 ESG report.

"We also have custom-developed a 40 percent postconsumer recycled PET (rPET) polyester water bottle pack liner. This now replaces virgin nylon material in 99 percent of our Gregory products." The decision, the company says, is diverting 1,632,960 plastic bottles every year from landfills.

The overall objective of these efforts?

To "continue to develop innovative solutions to ensure the durability of our products," the company wrote.

> "Eco innovations can be a really strong brand differentiator, especially in more developed markets. Overall, our priority is to increase the sustainability of our products while maintaining the quality and durability that our customers rightly expect."
>
> --Patrick Kwan
> Senior Director, Supply Chain Asia, Samsonite

The company is well on its way to achieving its 2030 Goal, which is to: "continue to develop innovative solutions to ensure the durability of our products, extend the life of our products, and develop viable end-of-life solutions to divert as many of our products from landfills for as long as possible. By using durable materials and increasing the life of our products, we are decreasing the burden on landfills," the ESG report noted.

And the company is doing that in two other ways as well.

"We are using recycled materials wherever possible, giving waste materials a second life." And "many/most of our products can be repaired worldwide so you won't need to replace them."

Three quick proof points to bring the idea home:

Since 2018, Samsonite has launched more than 50 luggage collections worldwide that have included a recycled material such as recycled PET (polyethylene terephthalate, the chemical name for polyester, and a clear, strong, and lightweight plastic), recycled nylon, post-industrial recycled polypropylene, wood waste, and cork.

Recyclex™, the fabric used for linings and soft-side bags, is made from 100 percent post-consumer recycled plastic bottles. So far, this has saved approximately 52 million 500ml plastic bottles from going to the landfill.

Then, there is something as simple as hangtags, the tag attached to a piece of merchandise that includes information about the manufacturer or designer, the fabric or material used, the model number, care instructions, and sometimes the price.

"All the hangtags on our Samsonite recycled collections are printed with soy ink, a sustainable alternative to traditional petroleum-based ink, made of paper from responsible sources and carry the Forest Stewardship Council (FSC®) logo," Miller says. "This standard provides an assurance that the paper used comes from well-managed FSC®-certified forests, recycled materials, and other controlled sources. In addition, we have removed the rubberized coating from the hangtags for our TUMI brand since it prevented them from being recyclable."

2) CARBON ACTION

Samsonite's approach to decreasing its "carbon footprint" is comprised of two parts: reducing emissions and increasing the efficiency of its manufacturing operations.

As the company writes in its ESG report, "we are working hard to minimize our impact on climate change and have set clear carbon reduction targets that mean we will be carbon neutral by 2025," when the company expects to be using 100 percent renewable energy.

You can see the progress the company is making.

The company reported that the production of finished goods increased by 60 percent from 2017 to 2019. Compared to 2017, when energy use increased by only two percent at manufacturing facilities, and greenhouse gas emissions decreased by four percent. This was made possible by on-site solar installations at manufacturing facilities in India and Belgium, energy efficiency upgrades across manufacturing centers, and economies of scale gained in production processes.

3) THRIVING SUPPLY CHAIN

It has been a long-time since Andrew Carnegie owned every step in his company's (steel) production process. (Carnegie died more than 100 years ago.)

Today, manufacturers invariably rely on others in producing their goods and getting them to market. Recognizing that fact, Samsonite has made optimizing the supply chain a key part of its ESG and CSR efforts to "encourage good practices and positive impacts beyond our direct business."

There are two major objectives. The company wants to make sure that: 1. All suppliers respect human rights and 2. All are engaging in responsible sourcing.

"Our suppliers are critical to the success of our business and we want to ensure that we work with like-minded partners: companies that share our values and our ethical way of working," says Paul Melkebeke, Samsonite's Chief Supply Officer. "We have robust policies and business codes in place to explain how we work and what is expected of our people and our suppliers, and we go to great lengths to check that these are being adhered to. This will help us to reach our pre-customer journey and human rights targets, ensuring we maintain our thriving supply chain in the years to come.

"We may have high expectations of our suppliers, but we expect them to have high expectations of us too," he adds. "Our Golden Rule, to treat others as we would like to be treated ourselves, extends to our supply chain; we always want our people to work in a straightforward, honest, and transparent way. We build relationships based on trust and mutual respect. Many last for years; some have been going for over three decades."

4) PEOPLE

It is easy to overlook the role that employees play in a company's sustainability efforts. But the reality is without employee engagement, nothing major is going to happen. That's true at every company, including Samsonite.

"First and foremost, on a practical level, I am a team of one," Miller says. "And so, I can't implement a global sustainability strategy without relying on my colleagues to do a lot of the heavy lifting. And a lot of the work, I just functionally can't do. I don't manage the machinery in our facilities. And so, I have no way of knowing how to improve the energy efficiency of those machines.

"I have to rely pretty heavily on my team to implement the strategy. And so, it's important from my perspective to have engagement," she adds. "Not just to say, 'Okay, it's a nice thing to do. I'll get to it when I get to it.' We need employees to say, 'This is important to my job. This is important to the company. This is important to me.'

"And I've been very fortunate at Samsonite to have a large

group of colleagues who are very committed to the work because they feel like not only is it important to the company, but they also feel it's important to them. Fundamentally, they understand the value of ESG personally and professionally."

> Companies don't do anything; their employees do. And if those employees don't feel engaged, the company will not be able to maximize its potential when it comes to sustainability, or anything else for that matter.

Samsonite's approach, when it comes to people, is focused on diversity and inclusion, as well as engagement and development.

WITH THE PLAN IN PLACE

Clear on its goals, the initial implementation steps included communicating the new sustainability strategy to external and internal audiences, including its global and regional sustainability committees and employees worldwide.

"So far, implementation has been going really well," Miller says. "The strategy development process required significant stakeholder engagement, and we are using the same approach toward developing implementation plans. Everyone at Samsonite is very engaged in, and committed to, the success of Our Responsible Journey."

Here's a quick example. "While we are still early in our strategy, we continue to expand our use of more sustainable materials in our products," Miller says. "You'll continue to see Recyclex™, our fabric made from recycled PET bottles, introduced in more product lines; 2020 saw the introduction of Clean Chroma®, a spin dying process that has fewer environmental impacts than traditional dying; and RapidFix™ repair kits that enable the consumer to make simple repairs to broken zippers on certain luggage lines, thereby extending the life of the luggage."

A SURPRISE

Speaking of durability, "we have had kind of an 'aha' moment about the connection between durability, repairability, and sustainability," Miller explains. "That's new among consumers since we started this effort. They didn't see the connection. Now they do.

"If you look at products that are not well-made, they break, they end up in a landfill, and then you have to replace them," which requires the use of more material and energy to produce the new item.

"When we realized that, we said 'hey, we have a product that is durable, it's made to be on the road or the trail with you as long as possible. Oh, and by the way, if it breaks, we also have this extensive network of repair centers, and we have some brands that will do repairs in store,'" Miller says. "So that no matter where you are, you can repair that product and continue on your way.

"We had this moment of, 'Oh, we've been doing this longer than we realized. And we've been committed to this before it even fit into that definition of sustainability.'"

GOING FORWARD

"I think it will be interesting to see if there is a rise in conscious consumerism post-pandemic," Miller says when asked about the future. "When you can't get out and shop as much as you used to, you start to realize the impact of human behavior on communities and the environment. You begin to think like, 'Oh, maybe the consumption mindset that I have isn't sustainable. How do I invest in items or belongings or things that are going to last? What are the categories of things that I should invest in? There might be some things I have been buying that aren't worth it. How do I think about well-made in a lot of different contexts?'"

Putting that comment in the context of the book, think about that old pair of jeans you have been wearing forever or that tote bag you have had for years, if not decades. You love these things because of the memories associated with them; that's what makes them relevant.

The fact that they have lasted this long—i.e., they are sustainable—is an added and treasured benefit. Well-worn doesn't mean worn out.

15

Kampgrounds of America

Change is Hard

Introducing a meaningful Diversity, Equity, and Inclusion mindset is necessary if your organization is going to be relevant (especially among younger generations) going forward. It is also extremely difficult to do.

Sir Isaac Newton's first law of motion is a bit wonky, given the way he wrote it: "Every object persists in its state of rest or uniform motion in a straight line unless it is compelled to change that state by forces impressed on it."

The way we learned it at school is simpler and clearer: "A body at rest will remain at rest, and a body in motion will remain in motion, unless it is acted on by an external force."

It boils down to this: Things will not start, stop, or alter direction by themselves. In other words, nothing changes unless it is forced to. Pushing a marble down an incline doesn't take much effort. Moving a boulder uphill requires a lot. But in either case, effort is required.

Why are we talking about physics? That's simple. There is no better way of describing the difficulty of instituting any change initiative. This is especially true when you want to make diversity, equity, and inclusion (DEI) an integral part of your corporate DNA.

And that is exactly the situation Kampgrounds of America

RELEVANCE

(KOA), the world's largest open-to-the-public campgrounds, faces going forward.

KOA AT A GLANCE

Kampgrounds of America (KOA) is the world's largest system of open-to-the-public campgrounds. (To understand why the first name of the company is spelled the way it is, see sidebar Why is Campgrounds spelled with a "K."

There are more than 520 KOA campgrounds in North America. There are KOA campgrounds in every U.S. state except Hawaii, Delaware, and Rhode Island and in every Canadian province other than Saskatchewan.

The company offers numerous camping options. Among them:

- **RV Sites** up to 120 feet, including pull-thrus, back-ins, and patio sites. They come complete with full hookups and WiFi.

- **Cabins.** The basic camping cabins, according to the company's website, "offer a cozy rustic experience with beds and stools. Many have upgraded amenities such as TVs and mini-fridges." Deluxe cabins offer full baths and bedrooms and may have a kitchen.

- **Tent camping** typically comes with picnic tables, water spouts, fire pits, restrooms, and showers nearby.

- **"Glamping."** The word, a combination of "glamorous" and "camping," the company says pairs "traditional camping elements of the past with the amenities of today."

President and CEO Toby O'Rourke wants DEI to be central to the mission of the almost 60-year-old company.

There are three reasons for that.

First, as she explains, it is simply the right thing to do.

"It is societally important," she says. "Every company should be taking a look at what they are doing in this space."

The second reason is to support a growing number of KOA customers who might otherwise feel uncomfortable and decide to go elsewhere.

"We do a lot of research, and we're seeing that increasingly there are more people of color, and under-represented communities, coming into camping," says O'Rourke. "Specifically, we've seen that 32 percent of campers now are from non-white or people of color communities, and that is a significant increase, an over 17-point increase, over the past five years. During my time here (O'Rourke joined the company in 2011 as KOA's digital marketing director), I've seen that number just continue to grow and grow and grow.

"And when we look at new campers who are just now coming into this lifestyle or activity, half are from those groups. So that's a very sizeable change in our industry, which has traditionally been Caucasian and older. We're seeing younger and more diverse campers."

That change is not quite as surprising as it first might appear.

"As more and more Millennials are coming in, we're seeing more and more diversity coming in," O'Rourke says. "As we broke down the research by age group, there were less differences among the Millennials no matter their race or ethnicity. The reasons they want to camp are similar. That wasn't the case among older generations."

RELEVANCE

The second reason ties to the first. As we saw back in Chapter 2, the need for DEI is something most Millennials believe in and endorse. We didn't ask the question directly in our research, but their preferences are clearly there by inference. We saw Millennials cited kindness and honesty as the two most important values required in dealing with the increase in racial tensions following the death of George Floyd and the rise of COVID-19. Of all the groups we surveyed, it was Millennials—by far—who said civil discourse is hard to come by today. Wholesale adoption of DEI efforts within all aspects of society, including business and organizations, can only help.

And that brings us to the third reason behind KOA's desire to make DEI a part of its corporate culture.

In 2018 "we had an incident, that was fueled by race, on a campground in Mississippi," O'Rourke explains. "A white employee of one of our franchisees—not an employee of KOA Incorporated and not the franchisee themselves—pulled a gun on an African-American couple who were picnicking by a lake on the property. They weren't registered guests, and she took that as they were trespassing. She said she pulled the gun because she was scared of the couple's dog. That was her angle. But no matter how you looked at it, it reflected poorly on the brand."

The Mississippi incident was an impetus to change. It jump-started KOA's work to cement DEI throughout the organization. Says O'Rourke: "That's when we started to be a lot more intentional about our work in this space."

WHERE THEY WERE. WHERE THEY ARE GOING

Before the incident in Mississippi, "I wouldn't say we're doing much to get a message out about our DEI efforts," O'Rourke says. "We've made a conscious effort to try to include more diversity in our marketing approach throughout my time here, showing all the kinds of people who camp with us, for example, but we weren't doing anything necessarily proactive about it, saying this is what KOA does when it comes to DEI.

"I guess the messaging was fine, but our DEI efforts are not about having a message. I really want to make a change in our organization. I mean, I'm not just doing something to tell people about it. I want to make meaningful change in the outdoor industry and in our organization.

"Here's one example of what that would look like for me. I would like to see more diversity in our franchisees. (Some 85 percent of the company's campgrounds are owned by franchisees.) We want to make a focused effort to bring more diverse people into our network that run campgrounds. I think that's important. And I also think that that's meaningful and actionable. It's not just to push a message out about how great KOA is.

"We definitely have representation across ethnic groups, also across LGBTQ," she adds. "And we're happy about that, but we have not done the work to say exactly what the percentages are. So that's part of what we're doing. We are going to gather the numbers and then set goals around that.

"I also want to spend time on our training. We're working right now on how we can better inform our campgrounds about customer service, with DEI layered in. Customer service is very important at KOA, but I don't think we've done a good job about layering DEI into our customer service efforts, so we're working through that. We are making efforts, and need to continue to do so, to show that we understand the importance of this work. It's not lip service. Lots of things are talked about. It's really action that means something."

How would that layering in of DEI work? O'Rourke provides a couple of examples.

"Language is very important," she says. "It can be as simple as taking out references in the descriptions of our properties to words like 'plantation' and 'antebellum architecture.' There's a lot of terminology, different vernacular, even different ways you may phrase something that could be taken offensively or viewed negatively.

"Here's an example, we had an incident where someone used the phrase 'you all' and it was taken to mean 'you and people like you.' The person it was said to, took 'you all' to mean the person talking was referring to all people of their race. That wasn't the intent, but that was what was heard. We're getting just a lot more conscious about how we use language. I don't think anyone's going out there and saying the really blatant, racist words. We are working on the language that could be taken poorly. We've learned a lot, and we're still learning and trying to learn about the differences and the nuances of the words we use.

"So that would be one way we are working DEI into customer

service," O'Rourke adds. "And it is important in de-escalating conflict. A conversation could begin as a standard customer service situation, but as the conflict escalates, whether that's through a poor use of language or an assumption made on either side, suddenly it turns into a racial discussion. We'll hear things like, 'Well, you're just saying that because I'm biracial,' or, 'You don't want my kid to do that,' even if there might be a rule being broken on the campground, 'because my daughter is Black.'

"In situations like this, everyone gets triggered, and people get very defensive, and then it just escalates from there," O'Rourke explains. "Since we have spent a lot of time thinking about our unconscious bias, we're now more attuned to that and what could happen. But I would guarantee most of our franchisees haven't thought about unconscious bias. So, we want to talk about that and also talk about what they are bringing to that situation that could cause it to escalate. Ultimately the question we want to ask is, 'how could you handle something like this differently?'

"This is something we work on at corporate as well."

> "We don't want to just pay lip service to this."
>
> --*Toby O'Rourke, CEO of KOA, talking about her company's DEI efforts.*

The fact that O'Rourke has been working to improve herself in this area makes an important point. The best way to get a message to resonate throughout the organization is for the leader to model the behavior she wants.

In O'Rourke's case, that meant saying, "we need to change. I am going to change."

And as you deliver the message, you need to be authentic.

What observers noticed after O'Rourke made her pledge to

stepping up KOA's commitment to DEI is that it opened up the discussion within the company about all their issues. Initially, there was a degree of fear among some people because they didn't want to say the wrong thing, or do something that might jeopardize their role, or make them look bad in any way. But O'Rourke helped them get over those concerns by basically saying, "you don't have to know everything, especially not going in, but you do need to participate in this. We're going to change."

And that eliminated people feeling like they were going to be left behind or saying the wrong thing. It took away the fear.

> "You can't just hang a sign in a window saying you believe in Diversity, Equity, and Inclusion and think it solves everything. There has to be action behind it."
>
> --Toby O'Rourke, CEO, KOA

"I think the reason there was fear stemmed from the customer service calls," O'Rourke says. "We were the ones getting backlash on social media if there's a poor experience. It was shocking to me we were getting so violently attacked by certain influencer groups who are very vocal in the space because I do think that we were making a conscious effort to handle every incident well. But since we are the biggest brand in camping, I get that we are going to take the brunt of a lot of it. It's par for the course of social media these days. There are always loud, very vocal groups and people who use an online platform to call brands on the carpet. That's okay because that's probably what needs to happen for change to happen. I take those charges very seriously.

"In 2020, we made the decision to ban the Confederate flag on our campgrounds after repeated pushback from many people," she adds by way of example. "It was starting to bubble up online.

Without that push, I'd like to say we would have gotten there on our own, but, in this case, I think someone calling you out and saying, 'How can KOA be better?' can help you move faster. It forced us to stop and have a conversation about it. Real change comes through sometimes very difficult conversations.

"I'm hoping these efforts that we're taking, and will take some time, will start to be recognized by people and that they will stay at KOA. We're making an effort, and I think it will make it more appealing to customers. We do have a great customer base, and a lot of times that's not recognized. I've seen a lot of it in my own experience here, and that is absolutely the case."

GOING FORWARD

Here's the company's plan going forward.

"We have plans across our human resources, our system development, our franchise services, and our marketing to tackle diversity, equity, and inclusion," O'Rourke says. "For example, I talked about increasing the number of non-white franchisees. And if we want to increase our franchise base, we need to then make sure that we have good representation on the franchise advisory board that meets with corporate and helps direct policies and how we operate. We need to make sure we have inclusion on that board. We are a minority-owned company. We're owned by Chinese Americans. The majority of the board is minority, but in our leadership ranks, we don't have that, and that's something we need to try to solve as well. We're also trying to work to make sure we have more women represented. We've got work to do to make sure we're inclusive and not making it just a face in the picture. People need to have a real seat at the table.

RELEVANCE

KOA'S HISTORY IS INTRIGUING

During the summer of 1962, hundreds of thousands, if not millions, of travelers passed through Billings, Montana, via U.S. 10 (this was years before Interstate 90 was built) on their way to the Seattle World's Fair.

"Local businessmen Dave Drum, John Wallace, and two partners set up a modest campground on Drum's property near what is now Riverfront Park just north of the Yellowstone River," the KOA website explains, to give these travelers a place to stop for a night or two.

"In exchange for the $1.75-per-night fee, travelers pitched their tents on a campsite outfitted with a picnic table and a fire ring. The campground offered a store, laundry facilities, and a hot shower."

The next year, Wallace mailed surveys to 500 customers to gather their impressions of their stay in Billings. What he discovered from the comments was there was a need for a nationwide network of modern campgrounds, and soon Kampgrounds of America was born.

"And I want the same kind of diversity, equity, and inclusion to exist in our partnerships, our creative, and our associations. For example, we are partners with Outbound Collective, an organization which describes itself this way: 'We're on a mission to get everyone outside.'*

"As a minority-owned and -operated business, we have a strong appreciation for the importance of building a community that reflects our society's diversity," O'Rourke says. "We believe that differences (of all kinds) make us stronger and more interesting. We are proud signatories of the Outdoor CEO Diversity Pledge, and we are committed to fostering an inclusive community that supports, elevates, and amplifies traditionally marginalized groups.

The Outdoor CEO Diversity Pledge connects leading outdoor brands with inclusion advocates to advance representation for people of color across the industry. We're focused on enhancing representation across staff and executive teams, media and marketing, and athletes/ambassadors. By building a relationship of support, empathy, and understanding, versus external skepticism and internal stress, we're moving the outdoor industry towards authentic inclusion.

"We're doing a lot of work here, and we're trying to sign on to be partners, not just in name, so that we can say we are, but to really get involved and try to bring more inclusivity to camping with people of color.

"I truly believe there's no better way for all races to connect than in the outdoors. It was hard for me to get my head around that some people don't feel welcome in the outdoors."

--*Toby O'Rourke, CEO, KOA*

"Our team really has a lot of passion for this work," O'Rourke says. "And when I say team, I'm talking about our leadership team, and teams within the home office. And sometimes, it's hard because, to make sure we're building the right plans and doing the right things, we sometimes have run into conflict with our franchise organization.

*This from their website: "We are a diverse community who shares an adventurous spirit. We yearn to get outside, reconnect, sweat, learn, and to have fun. We celebrate the simplicity and importance of everyday adventures, whether just down the street or across the globe. There is no after-work stroll too small, or far-off mountain too tall. We love all of it, and we welcome everyone who seeks the same. We're committed to building a movement that celebrates a more realistic and casual connection with the outdoors. One that is rooted in community, inclusion, everyday exploration, and inspiration."

RELEVANCE

"When you talk about bringing people together towards change, our franchise organization is like a snapshot of America. I realized that when we did the Confederate flag ban.

"I had some campground owners applauding us and excited about it. It makes their job easier on a campground to say, 'Hey, this is a corporate policy. You can't have a confederate flag up on your campsite.' Others felt that we were in violation of the constitution, and KOA was stepping on a political landmine. And we had some people who wanted to cancel their franchise agreement with us. So, uniting people is very difficult. In any issue we tackle, because we are so large, you are never going to have a hundred percent buy-in. And I have found that this DEI effort has been triggering for some people even going back to the incident in Mississippi.

"Because there was a gun involved, I had a lot of franchisees upset with me when we said that we didn't condone the use of guns at KOA. Some felt this violated their constitutional rights to bear arms.

"So, it's hard for us to bring our whole franchise system together for unity and to affect change. But if we ultimately believe it's the right thing to do, we will just keep moving forward, and that's what we're doing. It has not been easy. It's been probably the hardest thing I've done in my job, and I know it's just going to get even harder as we do more. We've got training scheduled for our convention this year, and I anticipate pushback from some people that we're bringing this topic up for discussion.

"I spoke at a camping conference last year, and had one slide in an 80-page slide deck that had a lot of logos of different groups, Black people camping and Hispanic, Latino, et cetera. And there was an LGBTQ group, and I had their logo up there, and it was triggering for someone who got very upset that I was advocating for LGBTQ people to be on our campgrounds.

"I think it's important that we try to be united, but the reality is we won't all be united, and I'm very grateful that I've got a team that believes in this and we're moving forward, even though it's very difficult," O'Rourke adds.

"It gets tiring. Sometimes I think the easy route would be to avoid this issue. But as CEO, you have to set an example. I try to apply morality to our decision-making here because, at the end of the day, it's not about just money. So, if we keep that lens on, I think that we can do the right thing."

16

In Conclusion, You Only Need to Ask One Question as You Navigate the Unknown

Are you relevant?

Everything we have talked about in the previous pages can be reduced to that question. More specifically, the question can be stated this way: Are you relevant to your customers and the people you would like to be your customers? Do you know enough about them to stay relevant in the months and years ahead amid what surely will be transformative changes, particularly digital ones?

Why is this question about relevance so important? Because if you answered in the negative, if you are not relevant, nothing else matters. You won't be able to get people to pay attention to either you or your message, and if they don't, there is no way that you will be able to influence their thoughts or behavior. All of your marketing and communication dollars will be wasted.

> If your product/service/idea resonates with a customer, if it means something to them—in addition to being utilitarian—then the relationship with the customer will be deeper, longer-lasting, and more profitable.

RELEVANCE

How do you know if you are relevant?

Your customers and potential customers will let you know by paying attention to what you have to say.

And that will only happen if you can get past the mental filters they have in place. Your message has to trigger one of the eight statements within the four quadrants below. After hearing your message, your audience needs to say your idea/product/service:

Thinking

• Helps me meet my needs.

• Makes my life easier.

Community

• Being associated with it makes me feel better about myself.

• I want people to know I am associated with it.

Values

• I associate the message/idea with values important to me.

• It stands for the same things I do.

Sensory

• I like the feeling when I'm around it.

• It inspires me.

If you can do that, if you can get past the filters, they will pay attention. If you can't, they won't.

How do you get past the filters?

Your starting point in forging a relationship with your customers and potential customers is understanding what is important to them. That way, you can interact with them through the lens which they view the world.

This means that every part of your communication efforts must contain at least one of the factors we talked about before; it must engage with people on a thinking, sensory, values, or community basis.

THINK BIGGER

As you go about trying to reach people, don't constrain yourself. Sure, you want to use the marketing techniques that have always served you well. But, as we saw throughout, they can be limiting.

Let's reprise an example that we used in Chapter 3.

Suppose your target audience is women 18-34 who have a household income of less than $50,000 a year. Within that demo, you have: female college and graduate students; women who stopped their formal education after senior year in high school and married early and have two or more children that they are raising at home; young women—some of whom are college graduates, some who are not—who are just getting their careers underway; and women who have decided to leave the workforce for a while to have their first child. You get the idea. It is hard to find a common denominator, especially once you factor in that some of the women live on farms and rural areas, others in big cities like Chicago, Los Angeles, or New York and the rest in the suburbs. The fact is that two 26-year-old women—the mid-point of your demo—can be extremely different, and a one-size-fits-all approach is not going to work if you are trying to get them to pay attention to what you have to say or sell. The message that resonates with one may not resonate with the other.

That's why we strongly advocate for searching out tribes and adding marketing clusters to your mix. (See our discussion in Chapters 4-5.)

RELEVANCE

RELEVANCE IN A TIME OF UNCERTAINTY

As we write this at the end of November 2020, we have just finished a grueling presidential election where 81,282,495 voters (52.2%) ended up happy, and the other 74,223,755 (47.8%) were not. When the margin of victory in an election where more than 150 million votes were cast is less than 5 percent, you don't need us to point out just how divided the country is. On a bright note, it looks like a successful vaccine against COVID-19 will be available within weeks.

No one knows what the world will look like going forward.

But we do know this: Now more than ever, your message needs to be relevant, or you simply won't be heard. Relevance will differentiate you from your competition, increasing your odds of success.

Epilogue: A Brighter Future

Following the 2020 presidential election, we surveyed high-to-mid level professionals to better understand how the election results will affect their business decisions and priorities. We were reassured by what we found.

For example, about three out of four executives believe the election will have a positive impact in both the short and long term.

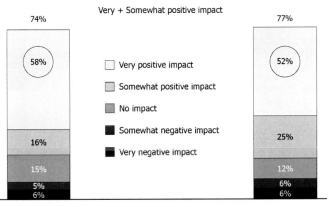

Election's Impact on Business
Short-term vs. Long-term

How do you think the results of the 2020 presidential election will impact your business in the short-term and your long-term business strategy?

Question Type: Single Choice | Total Respondents: 351

Very + Somewhat positive impact

74% 77%

□ Very positive impact
▨ Somewhat positive impact
▦ No impact
■ Somewhat negative impact
■ Very negative impact

58% 52%

16% 25%

15% 12%

5% 6%
6% 6%

Short-term impact Long-term impact

RELEVANCE

Business leaders agree the results of the 2020 election will have a positive impact on their businesses' short-term and long-term strategies.

In the short-term, well over half of business leaders say the election will have a very positive impact.

Similarly, half of business leaders believe the election will have a very positive impact on their business long-term.

Few believe there will be a negative impact on their business in the short-term or the long-term.

A major reason for that confidence, of course, is their belief in the new president's ability to handle the major issues our country faces.

Confidence in President-Elect Biden

As a result of the 2020 presidential election, are you more or less confident in each of the following?

Question Type: Single Matrix | Total Respondents: 351

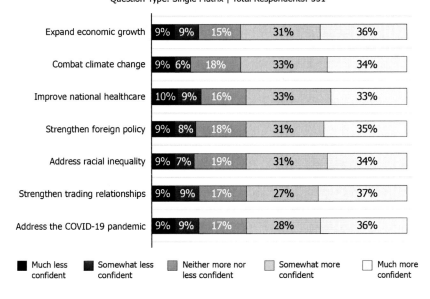

	Much less confident	Somewhat less confident	Neither more nor less confident	Somewhat more confident	Much more confident
Expand economic growth	9%	9%	15%	31%	36%
Combat climate change	9%	6%	18%	33%	34%
Improve national healthcare	10%	9%	16%	33%	33%
Strengthen foreign policy	9%	8%	18%	31%	35%
Address racial inequality	9%	7%	19%	31%	34%
Strengthen trading relationships	9%	9%	17%	27%	37%
Address the COVID-19 pandemic	9%	9%	17%	28%	36%

Confidence in President-Elect Biden trends positively across key issues.

More than a third of business leaders are much more confident in President-elect Biden's ability to strengthen and expand core tenets of business growth—expanding economic growth and strengthening trading relationships.

RELEVANCE

Not surprisingly, given the first two points, the leaders we talked to said they were confident it would be a bit easier for them to run their businesses going forward.

Confidence in Business Post-Election

As a result of the 2020 presidential election, are you more or less confident in each of the following?

Question Type: Single Matrix | Total Respondents: 351

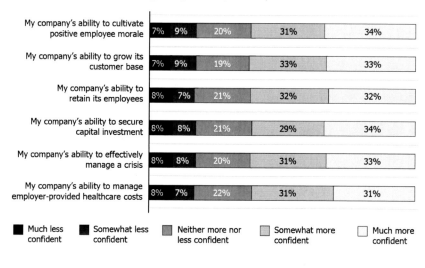

Business leaders are generally more confident in things their company is able to control—such as employees and growing customers.

Two-thirds of business leaders are more confident in their company's ability to cultivate positive employee morale, grow its customer base, and retain employees.

Epilogue

However, they told us that inside their organizations, some things are probably going to change.

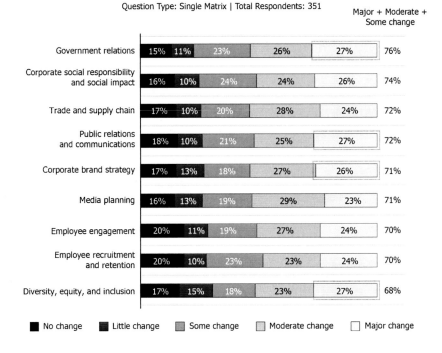

Shifting Priorities and Changes

As a result of the 2020 presidential election, how much change do you expect your organization will need to make in each of the following business areas?

Question Type: Single Matrix | Total Respondents: 351

Major + Moderate + Some change

Business area	No change	Little change	Some change	Moderate change	Major change	Total
Government relations	15%	11%	23%	26%	27%	76%
Corporate social responsibility and social impact	16%	10%	24%	24%	26%	74%
Trade and supply chain	17%	10%	20%	28%	24%	72%
Public relations and communications	18%	10%	21%	25%	27%	72%
Corporate brand strategy	17%	13%	18%	27%	26%	71%
Media planning	16%	13%	19%	29%	23%	71%
Employee engagement	20%	11%	19%	27%	24%	70%
Employee recruitment and retention	20%	10%	23%	23%	24%	70%
Diversity, equity, and inclusion	17%	15%	18%	23%	27%	68%

■ No change ■ Little change ▨ Some change ▨ Moderate change ☐ Major change

RELEVANCE

Over a quarter of business leaders say they expect major changes in external-facing strategies like government relations, public relations, and corporate brand strategy.

There are also anticipated changes to DEI and CSR— over a quarter say their organization will need to make major changes in these areas.

As we said, we are optimistic about the future.

About the Author

Andrea "Andy" Coville is CEO of Brodeur Partners, one of the world's top mid-sized communications agencies. In a quest to bring more science and sensory-based insight to the creative process, she developed and refined the concept of relevance, a strategic platform for helping organizations and their brands go beyond the "buzz" and link communications to behavioral change.

For 30 years, she has executed high-performing relevance campaigns for organizations in the business-to-business, consumer products, and healthcare markets. Her agency's extensive client roster has included the American Cancer Society, IBM, Mastercard, Corning, Philips, BlackBerry, Bio, Vertex, 3M, Dartmouth College, Fidelity Investments, Hankook Tire, and AMOREPACIFIC.

After joining Brodeur in 1986 and becoming CEO in 1999, Andy diversified Brodeur Partners from a public relations firm specializing in technology to a multidisciplinary communications agency focusing on full-service communications, digital strategies, social change, and business consulting. During that process, she oversaw the acquisition of companies that expanded the agency's portfolio in diversity and inclusion, social purpose, digital and video, paid social, and branding.

Andy has a bachelor's degree in journalism and English literature from the University of New Hampshire. She is married to John Brodeur (co-founder of Brodeur Partners), is a mother of four, and has a passion for social causes that advance the well-being of children. She serves on several nonprofit boards and is an avid running and outdoor sports enthusiast.